D1286350

IRON MEN

IRON MEN

A Saga of the Deputy United States Marshals
Who Rode the Indian Territory

C. H. McKENNON

1967

DOUBLEDAY & COMPANY, INC., GARDEN CITY, NEW YORK

To MIKE and SANDY

As with all children————
they will face frontiers
of their own—————

WHY DID THEY DO IT?
By William P. Robinson

Indeed, why did any man ever want to serve as a United States deputy marshal, to police an undeveloped frontier peopled with an unco-operative—sometimes hostile—citizenry, to live in constant danger for little or no pay?

The question is more rhetorical when we remember the turbulent years after the Civil War. Federal law enforcement in the Western District of Arkansas, which included all the area that later became Oklahoma, presented almost insuperable difficulties. The ordinary drudgery of detecting evidence, tracking down and apprehending the criminal was expected and accepted. Danger surprised no one. But even when a dollar grew bigger than a wagon wheel, the U.S. deputy marshal could hope for little more than reimbursement for expenses. A parsimonious governmental policy allowed him fees on a "when-and-if" basis.

The "iron men" didn't expect riches; adventure was easy to come by without being a deputy marshal. Fame? Even an "iron man" can't eat it! Nevertheless, men came forward to do a necessary job—"men who were willing to take risks to have law and order established." Federal Judge Isaac Parker, "Hanging Judge," drew to Fort Smith and into federal service this kind of man. C. H. McKennon's history adds an important, long-neglected chapter to the epic of these incredible Spartans, the "iron men"—Paden Tolbert, John N. Sarber, Logan Roots, Heck Thomas, Dave Rusk, and many other lawmen who performed far beyond the call of duty.

Curiously enough, a whole platoon of these deputy marshals grew to manhood in or near "Bloody Clarksville," Arkansas, a real crime center during the uncertain and troublous Reconstruction period after the close of the Civil War. Into this rough environment in 1880, James R. Tolbert, journalist and peach fancier, brought his family from Georgia. His son Paden was then a boy of eighteen. Young Paden in his adolescent years saw the successful labors of Sheriff "Bud" McConnell turn "Bloody Clarksville" into a safe, law-abiding community. And as a young man, Paden Tolbert learned the rudiments of his trade serving as a posseman and deputy sheriff under Sheriff McConnell. *Iron Men* is Tolbert's story, but it is also a vivid account of the achievements of others like him.

The names of lawbreakers are here, too. Familiar names like Sid Wallace, Ned Christie, Bill Doolin, "Cherokee Bill" Goldsby, Bill and Jim Cook, and Al Jennings. But in this fresh contribution to western Americana, these criminals are stripped of folklore and legend. The impartial light of history dispels all vestiges of pseudo-romantic disguise.

Mr. McKennon artfully weaves into his writing the folk vocabulary of the late nineteenth century southwestern *mise en scène*. He achieves this difficult task so smoothly that the reader quite often feels that a contemporary of the "iron men" is telling the tale. Frequently in this history of half-forgotten exploits, one does get his information almost firsthand from conversations reported in diaries or from men who were there or from descendants of Paden Tolbert and other deputy marshals, corroborated, of course, by public records.

One of the chief contributions to our lore in *Iron Men* is C. H. McKennon's account of the crimes of Ned Christie, never previously written completely for the general reader. Christie was a highly respected Cherokee Indian who began a criminal career by unwittingly murdering a deputy U.S.

marshal one night in Tahlequah, Cherokee Nation. As lawmen repeatedly failed to bring Christie to justice, he graduated from murder to lesser crimes of robbery and arson, meanwhile building himself a well-nigh impregnable fort on a hill fourteen miles east of Tahlequah. Mr. McKennon collects all the facts, showing how Paden Tolbert's leadership and bulldog persistence finally closed the chapter with Ned Christie's violent death when he, fully in character, resisted arrest to the end.

Perhaps each of us today owes it to himself to look into *Iron Men* and find the answer to this question, "Why did they do it?" Without its "iron men" of every crucial period, America could not have made it to mid-twentieth century. Certainly today's problems of national defense and security will be solved by iron men, and future crises will unquestionably bring forward their modern knights errant on horseback in support of the old-fashioned virtues of honesty, integrity, loyalty, and devotion to duty.

". . . When deputy marshals imposed law and order in the wild Indian Territory, there was a lot of imposing to do. It was in the days before fingerprints and a man could change his whisker style as easily as he could his name. The "New Lands" were filled with fugitives and outlaws, and the man who traveled horseback across the Territory slept on his gun in an open place, and tried not to sleep too soundly.

Obviously, a business and agricultural civilization couldn't make much headway until the era of casual murder and open plunder was over.

The builder-type lived a quiet life, concerned with cattle raising, banking, chamber of commerce work and civic problems. He was perhaps an unspectacular pioneer—devoted, hard working and laboring for the best interests.

Of the two types script-writers would infinitely prefer the lawman. But taming a country is like taming a horse. It means nothing until you begin riding the horse on purposeful errands.

Oklahoma's builders took the mustangs that the lawmen broke and rode them well on chores necessary to build up the new country.

We are in debt to the lawmen and the builders, and we are saddened when they go."

From an editorial on the passing Oklahoma Pioneers—by Jenkin Lloyd Jones, Editor—the Tulsa Tribune.

CONTENTS

LIST OF ILLUSTRATIONS

(Following page 104)

1

RAILS WESTWARD

Two young men stood quietly on the station platform, captivated by a huge, hissing railroad locomotive that towered over them. High above their heads, the engine's great, bulbous stack emitted a trail of grayish-black wood smoke.

With the aplomb that only an older brother can muster at times, though only two years separated their ages, eighteen-year-old Paden Tolbert explained the working parts to John. The rather pleasant odors of wood smoke, hot metal, and heated cylinder oil were alien to the nostrils of the boys, and it served to increase their awe of the monster. The ponderous driver wheels towered above their heads, and they tried to visualize the tremendous power that was latent in the steam cylinders and drive rods. From deep within the iron bowels of the giant, a mysterious rumble could be heard.

"Maybe," Paden whispered to himself, "I'll be a railroad engineer."

Farther down the wooden station platform the rest of the Tolbert family were waiting near the passenger coach entrance. James Russell Tolbert puffed his cheroot nervously, and as habit asserted itself, he used the slender cigar as a pointer to quickly count noses of his family. His wife was gently rocking a hooded wooden-wheel perambulator that contained David, the youngest of her family of seven boys and a daughter. Holding tightly to his mother's free hand was two-year-old Eugene, appearing uncomfortable in his new middy blouse and shoes. Vernon, Harry, and Charles, ranging in age from thirteen to eight, were engrossed in the activities of the telegraph agent, visible through the large bay window of his office as he busily worked his key. Five-year-old Maggie was contentedly sorting the contents of her small carpetbag, bought especially for the journey.

Casting his eyes around the platform, J. R. Tolbert located his two older sons standing beside the locomotive. He struck a match on the sole of his boot and puffed his cheroot to new life. The boys, he could see, were still bubbling with the adventure of "the trip." Even the long ride from Georgia to Little Rock, Arkansas, had not dulled their interest. They had fretted during the transition from Little Rock, across the Arkansas River, to Argenta (present-day North Little Rock), a necessary interruption of the rail trip in order to board another train on the distant bank of the river. Now, the boys were eager to climb on the new train that would carry them farther westward.

Losing interest in the telegrapher, Charles clambered atop a high-wheel baggage cart. From his vantage perch he could see inside the waiting coach.

"It's got fuzzy red seats," he shrilly proclaimed.

"Land of Goshen, Charley," chided Mrs. Tolbert, "stop your shrieking, the driver will think it's the whistle and he'll drive off without us."

"He's not a driver, Momma," corrected Charles, "he's the engineer and *he* blows the whistle."

"All right, Charles," smiled his mother, "but get down, I know we'll be starting soon."

Elizabeth Peden Tolbert was outwardly serene in her best green velvet dress with balloon sleeves, tight bodice, and long, swirling skirts. She was concealing her anxiety well. One more loading and she figured that her fine china would have a chance to survive the long journey westward. She reached out and gently pulled away a wisp of straw that protruded from the lid of a wooden hogshead. The cylindrical crate contained her precious chinaware—remnants of gracious living "before the war." She placed the bit of straw in the tousled locks of her youngster.

"Little Mr. Straw Man," she proclaimed, and the little boy laughed.

J. R. Tolbert was none too successful in hiding his restlessness. He pulled his beaver hat from his head and gave his thick, brown hair, which was beginning to gray, a combing with his fingers. Despite his air of self-assurance he knew that his family was pulling deep roots in migrating to a place that was undergoing rather violent changes. The family's two large trunks had been deposited on the platform near the china crate, and Tolbert sat his large frame down on the rounded top of one of them. At once, though, the locomotive gave a strident, warning blast with its whistle, and he bounded to his feet. Interrupted in their mechanical inspection by the loud whistle, the two older boys trotted down the platform to join their parents.

"The engine fireman threw enough cordwood on his fire to last our ole' kitchen stove a week," John announced importantly.

"My, my," exclaimed his mother, pleased with the interest her boys were displaying, "it must cost those railroad people a tidy sum just for firewood."

A colored baggageman tipped his cap to Mrs. Tolbert and carefully tilted the family's hogshead. Securing a firm hold on the bottom rim, he straightened with a mighty heave and deposited the cask on his shoulder. He marched down the platform to the baggage coach, expertly balancing his heavy load.

Mrs. Tolbert breathed a sigh of relief as the china barrel disappeared through the gaping door of the baggage coach. At least, she thought, the family would arrive with everything it had commenced the trip with. She superintended the placing of the perambulator aboard and then took a firm hold on little Eugene's hand, primly gathered her skirts, and permitted the conductor to assist her into the passenger coach. The remainder of her brood followed, and her husband was the last to swing aboard. The Tolbert family was on the last leg of its journey.

With bell clanging and smokestack belching huge volumes of smoke, the locomotive began a majestic, slow movement, pulling the short string of coaches out of the Argenta station. Paden and John found an open window, and they immediately took full possession of the valuable site, ignoring an occasional spray of ashes and soot. They had discovered on the previous leg of the trip that, by poking their heads out the window, they could have a splendid view of the chuffing locomotive when it was on a curve that favored their window.

J. R. Tolbert tossed his hat on the wire net shelf above the car seats and eased his bulk down beside his wife. He placed the small boy on his lap as Mrs. Tolbert arranged the perambulator that was parked in the narrow aisle. She placed a large wicker basket on her lap and removed its white linen cover. She began sorting thick slices of bread and yellow cheese that the basket contained. Tolbert smiled as his wife began to hum snatches from her favorite hymn, an old "kitchen" habit she had back in Georgia. Her improving spirits delighted him, for she had been glum the day they had packed for the trip. Tolbert accepted a piece of cheese as his mind went back to his beloved Georgia. The lad in his lap promptly appropriated the morsel as his father drifted into a reverie.

Georgia had been all but destroyed in the war. The battles of Peachtree Creek and Ezra Creek, not to mention the Battle of Atlanta, had been preludes to Sherman's devastating march to the sea. A swath thirty miles wide had been laid waste all the way to Savannah. In the shorn area a house could not be found intact. Railroads were knocked out and some of the rails were uprooted and twisted around tree trunks. Wagon roads, chewed into deep ruts by military use, were impassable. And it was a silent area where not a single chicken could be heard cackling, nor a vestige of crops seen, or any evidence of livestock.

Tolbert thought of a remark he had read somewhere about the rubble that was Atlanta when the war ended.

"Hell has laid her egg, and right here it hatched."

The phrase intrigued his journalistic instinct, just as the devastation of agriculture in the country had made his heart sick. Not only had town and country changed, but the very core of the social order had been destroyed. And the violent changing had not ceased with Lee's surrender in 1865.

The postwar federal government instituted a system of reconstruction that was designed to recreate loyal state governments. Secessionists had lost all seats in the new political structure, and of course, in any official voice in affairs. Atlanta had been rebuilt with amazing rapidity, but the countryside was much slower in recovering from the rape of war.

Considered "well-fixed" before the war, Tolbert was a graduate of the University of Georgia at Athens, and of a law school in Tennessee. He had married one year before the outbreak of hostilities, and his future appeared secure. Then came the war and the crumbling of his estate near Griffin, Georgia. His family lived sporadically in Macon and in Atlanta during the war years, following him in his newspaper work. He attempted farming in Pike County and his efforts as a columnist for the Atlanta *Constitution* were rewarding—as a medium for editorializing—but monetarily, the career could not halt the decay of his estate.

Most of the southern states were readmitted to the Union by 1868, but Georgia, as a result of its turmoil and chaos, was not adjudged ready until 1870. The ensuing decade brought little encouragement for Tolbert. With the dawning of 1880 and with his oldest of seven sons fast approaching young manhood, he decided on a drastic move.

"I'll find a small-town newspaper for sale—further west," he announced to his startled wife.

The only really convincing argument that had swayed his wife was the apparent lack of a future for their children. The estate had brought just enough funds to make the rail journey to a small town in western Arkansas, and to purchase a newspaper establishment Tolbert had spotted in a *Constitution* ad.

"Well, Georgia is sho' a fair piece behind us," Tolbert announced to his wife, as he reached in the basket for a chunk of the home-made bread. "And, this leg of the trip will put us in Clarksville—practically at the end of the track."

Paden overheard his father's remark. "End of the track!" The term sounded adventurous. It foretold of a distant place where things were happening, where towns would be growing and exciting instead of becoming weedy and run-down. Paden knew that his mother had voiced objections to the move. Long before the the actual trip had begun there were grown-up discussions—when the younger children were not supposed to be listening—and Paden, as the eldest boy, had voiced his approval. However, he had heard his mother worriedly question his father about "shootings" and a "hanging on the public square." Was this place a frontier? The destination was becoming as exciting as the thrill of "riding the cars." He gazed from his coach window and noted that the track right-of-way did have a raw appearance as compared to the older railroads they had been traveling.

As the rocking train clickety-clacked mile after mile along the rails, young Paden's curiosity mounted. More and more from his window view, the right-of-way appeared to have been recently constructed. Finally, the cuts and passes in the rolling countryside showed a naked countenance, almost devoid of even the ambitious Jimson weed and Bermuda grass.

"Daddy," queried Paden Tolbert, "what's this town of Clarksville really like—?"

2

MURDER IN THE CIVIL WAR

Three unkempt, blue-clad cavalrymen urged their horses into the dimness of a covered bridge. Although the muffled thunder of the horses' hoofs reverberated up the dusty main street of Clarksville, Arkansas, the sounds of traffic caused no undue interest. The year of 1863 was drawing to a close, and the little city had been occupied for some time by Yankee soldiers. Troops of Company C, 2nd Kansas Regiment, surged everywhere in precise military confusion, preoccupied with the business of patrols.

The rumbling within the covered bridge at the west end of Main Street ceased as the riders emerged into the sunlight of a mild winter day. As the group put spurs to their mounts and galloped up a hill that rose from the east end of the bridge, a keen-eyed observer on the narrow path that bordered the steep road noted the shoddiness of the men.

The original "spit and polish" had long since rubbed off the seasoned soldiers garrisoned in the town, but their accouterments and personal appearances reflected the hawk-eyed surveillance of Lieutenant Gideon M. Waugh. The three horsemen leaving the town did not, by any stretch of the imagination, reflect Lieutenant Waugh's conception of well-turned-out cavalrymen.

Leaving the echoes of the covered bridge behind them, the riders topped "East Hill." One, a hulking brute who dwarfed the horse he was riding, was decked out in an infantryman greatcoat—several sizes too small. A much smaller man was astride a farm saddle instead of the neat cavalry issue. The third horseman was an average-sized fellow, but his shoulders were extremely narrow, and a shotgun instead of the regulation carbine was shoved in his saddle boot. All three men wore ragged beards that obviously had not been trimmed for some time. However, the mounts of the hard-bitten trio were excellent, the best obtainable in the Southland by force.

Lieutenant Waugh, whose convincing front of metallic bravado hid a soul deathly sick of the dreariness of war, would have ordered the men to fatigue duty on the dung heaps of the company corral if he had encountered them. The lieutenant, though, was up to his ears with company worries. From his window of the frame courthouse where headquarters had been set up, he glowered at the shabby fronts of store buildings facing the street.

"If those damn buildings weren't so dingy," the lieutenant muttered, "the place would look like a cavalry post."

Only an occasional civilian could be seen on the streets. The blue-clad figures of soldiers completely dominated the scene.

The lieutenant sighed. "Reckon they carry on their little businesses by ducking in and out of back doors."

The courthouse dominated a square situated in the middle of the town. From his vantage point the lieutenant surveyed a dismal scene. Food was scarce. It was December 31, and his men six days ago had celebrated Christmas. The troopers marked the day by gnawing on moldy hardtack biscuits and slices of rubbery steak from a sick old cow that had been lassoed and butchered. The Methodist Church across the street from the southwest corner of the square had been converted to a commissary by the Yankees. A quick examination that morning had revealed that supplies were dangerously low.

"Damn," growled the lieutenant, turning from the window.

The young cavalryman eyed an array of telegraphic equipment in a corner of the chilly room. Before the occupation the room had served as the town's telegraph office. Now the instruments were somberly quiet. The apparatus had proven to be of negligible value to the federal troops. They were not able to maintain the lines to either Fort Smith or Little Rock. Wires were mysteriously cut almost as soon as a break was located and repaired. One wire snipper had been observed more than once, but always the elusive guerrilla had quickly mounted a splendid white horse and easily outdistanced the angrily pursuing cavalrymen. And the red-faced horsemen were forced to report to Lieutenant Waugh that the agile quarry was a wisp of a girl.

The lieutenant slid a watch from underneath his tunic and frowned. An hour ago he had a courier pounding down the narrow road to Little Rock. It would be, he thought, two days before the rider could complete the 200-mile round trip. Exchanges of fresh mounts along the way were likely to be sparse. Even after the command at Little Rock received the dispatch from the Clarksville garrison there would be a delay. The urgently requested food supplies would be piled aboard the next Union steamboat westbound up the Arkansas River.

The lieutenant snapped the face of his watch shut and returned the timepiece to his inside coat pocket.

"Damn," he muttered. "Damn this war all to hell."

The three horsemen on East Hill swung their mounts to the right and took the road to Cabin Creek, a town five miles distant. They had watched Lieutenant Waugh's courier thunder through the covered bridge in town, and they knew that the Little Rock road would not be likely to have further military travel for a few hours. However, the riders were not bound for Little Rock, or even the nearby town of Cabin Creek. Two miles out of Clarksville they reined up in front of a large, comfortable dwelling. The house was built of heavy, carefully hewn logs. A massive stone chimney loomed above the center point of the ridge pole, and a thin wisp of blue wood smoke trailed lazily upward. A neat wooden rail fence paralleled the road and enclosed a large front yard.

One of the riders leaned in his saddle and fumbled with the wire loop that secured the hinged front gate.

"Hell fire," snorted the big man, "let's call the old boy out here."

"Hey, preacher, c'mon out hyar," bawled the man at the gate.

The Reverend Vincent M. Wallace opened his front door and stepped out on the narrow porch.

"We ain't aiming to trespass none," the huge horseman said with exaggerated courtesy, "but we got a question to put to ye."

"Reckon there be ary men in thet house," nervously whispered the rider with the narrow shoulders.

"Hell," snapped the burly horseman who evidently was the leader, "don't reckon there be ary gun-bearing age kid left in this hull county—let alone a man."

Reverend Wallace stepped down from his porch and approached the group at the gate.

The three horsemen eyed the minister intently. The man's hands were empty and his shirt, a loosely fitting garment of rough cloth, was not full enough to conceal a revolver. The minister's trousers, supported by wide leather galluses, were neatly fitted to his muscular legs and were threadbare to the point of bursting at the knees. By the time he had reached the gate the horsemen knew that he was not armed.

"We hear tell you'ins got money buried," said the big rider bluntly, leaning slightly in his saddle to elaborately expectorate an amber stream of tobacco juice.

The sun in the west was colliding with the horizon. The yellowing light tinted the graying hair of Reverend Wallace as his face reflected his astonishment. He knew that no one in town—including himself—had had more than a dribble of "hard money" in the past year.

"Son," said the minister, "I am afraid that you have been misinformed. I have no money in my pockets—let alone buried."

The assumed air of casualness left the big man. His coarse black eyebrows narrowed to a straight line, and his lips twisted in a snarl.

"Dig hit up!"

The minister spread out his arms. "But, men—"

The rider with the scrawny shoulders jerked his shotgun from the scabbard and thrust the twin muzzles against the preacher's lips.

"Dig hit up," the ruffian growled, aping his leader, and then, to lend importance to his demand, he uttered a fearful volley of unadulterated mule-barn cursing.

The minister's gray eyes bored into the flushed face of the narrow-shouldered man.

The calm dignity of Wallace shattered the grubby soldier's shaky poise. He regretted making the demand, for now the attention of the group was focused on him. And, from the corner of his eye he became aware that two women had appeared in the doorway of the Wallace home. The additional audience stirred his anger, and his mind formed a soundless oath. Finally, the level gaze of the preacher infuriated him. Just as the leader swelled his enormous chest to bark an impatient order, the shotgunner pulled both triggers.

The sudden bellow of the gun sent long, rolling echoes mumbling across the late afternoon countryside. The big horseman was gaping at the bloody form of the minister that had been hurled to the ground by the impact of the double shot.

"Hell fire," he suddenly roared, "whut did ye go and do that fur! We could'a worked him over some."

The ruddiness of the shotgunner's faced melted away to a pasty white. His bluster vanished.

"I'm a-gettin outa hyar," he gasped, grabbing up his reins with his free hand. Wheeling his horse, he cruelly jabbed spurs in the excited animal. Instantly man and beast were flying down the road, the rider frantically clubbing the horse's rump with the shotgun.

The third horseman, wild-eyed with sick fear, made no comment as he put his mount into a full gallop after his fleeing companion.

The big man, his horse prancing and pitching with wall-eyed excitement, hurled a scorching barrage of cavalry oaths at his disappearing cronies. Realizing the futility of words, he cast a quick glance at the stunned women in the doorway, and then at the prone body of the minister. His coarse face flamed with rage as he savagely dug his mount into a dead run eastward on the Cabin Creek road, and he thundered away in hot pursuit of his distant companions.

Sydney Wallace, age twelve, heard the loud, coarse shouts out on the road that paralleled the Wallace front yard. His mother and "Aunt Missouri" Blackard, the slave woman who had been in the Wallace home as long as Sid could remember, had gone to the open front door. Blue-clad soldiers passing along the road, or even stopping to ask questions, were nothing unusual. But the oaths he heard were new around the Wallace home. He had heard a few "cuss words" that were uttered by his companions at the little schoolhouse over toward town, but such words at home—never! It was a strange world for a twelve-year-old boy. The coming of the Yankees had changed everything.

Curiosity compelled Sid to go to the front door. He peered around the ballooning skirts of Aunt Missouri. Just as his eyes took in the scene of three horsemen on the outside of the fence and the familiar figure of his father, the rude roar of a shotgun assaulted his ears. Inquisitiveness turned to horror as he saw his father knocked to the ground as though struck by a giant invisible fist.

Sid was only dimly aware of the aftermath shouts, and the drumming hoofbeats that followed the echoes of the shotgun blast. He did not notice his mother—rapidly slipping into a state of shock—begin to wring her hands violently. He saw only the dreadfully still figure of his father.

When Lieutenant Gideon M. Waugh awoke the next morning, an orderly informed him of the murder of Vincent Wallace. The lieutenant braced himself to face an angry town, but he was totally unprepared for the white-hot rage of the citizens.

Wallace was a Methodist minister, and though he had a church at Greenbriar, a settlement a few miles north of Cabin Creek, he often rode a circuit. From 1848 to 1850 he had served as surveyor of Johnson County. He became a well-known figure in northwestern Arkansas when he was elected to appear in the ninth session of the state legislature, serving in 1852 and '53 as representative from Johnson County. In 1861, when the clouds of war became visible, he was a member of a committee appointed by a board of Johnson County citizens to spend $500 for powder, lead shot, and caps. When the war came, Clarksville, as with other towns in the South, was quickly stripped of able-bodied men and youths. The Reverend Wallace had marched away to war, but he had been furloughed home to see about his family. Also, he was something of a minister without portfolio to check on the families of the men of his regiment. There were tales of extreme hardship—which Wallace's officers suspected were exaggerated—that needed to be checked. Clarksville was occupied by the enemy and with Wallace's rating of ministry, it was thought that he would make an ideal envoy.

Wallace had been considered a well-to-do man in the community until the hungry fingers of war plucked everything but the bare rudiments of his Clarksville farm. It was the former solvency, Lieutenant Waugh assumed, that accounted for the robbery attempt resulting in the murder of Wallace. The bitterness of the people in the Confederate bastion that was Clarksville astounded the lieutenant.

Old-timers in town told for years to come the dressing down the lieutenant received when he stepped out onto the court square that New Year's day of 1864. A furious, white-haired old man was waiting for him. Lieutenant Waugh was tongue-lashed to a fare-thee-well with "you and your goddam blue-bellied cutthroats—"

Lieutenant Waugh, and Major Marshall L. Stephenson of the 10th Illinois Cavalry, also stationed at Clarksville, ordered a thorough investigation. As soon as he obtained descriptions of the three horsemen, Lieutenant Waugh doubted that he would ever see their faces, and he proved to be something of a prophet. The investigation never did establish whether the three horsemen involved in the murder of Wallace were soldiers or renegades camouflaged in the blue uniforms of the North. The difficulties Waugh faced in this respect were understood by the citizens of Clarksville, for the practices of Quantrill and his guerrilla band were not uncommon in Johnson County. To the north, only 120 miles, was the southern boundary of Missouri, and to the west, the Indian Territory was only 65 miles distant.

The men of the Kansas Regiment were not above hooking a cow from the pasture of an unwary farmer and butchering it at the nearest convenient place. They would dismount and give wild chase at the mere glimpse of an unfortunate chicken. Well aware of these practices, Lieutenant Waugh would periodically assemble the men for lecture. It was a difficult job for the lieutenant, for he knew that the pangs of hunger prompted the depredations.

An old farmer from the west side of town had bitterly

complained to the lieutenant of the theft of an iron pot full of bubbling hominy. A group of cavalrymen had lassoed the heavy pot and dragged it away from the fire when the old man had stepped inside his house. Lieutenant Waugh found the iron pot emptied of its contents and had it returned to the farmer.

The incident prompted a lecture. Lieutenant Waugh addressed his men with good military bellowing, outlining the type of punishment that would befall any soldier caught molesting civilian property. The lieutenant was not a man to take lightly, and his warnings had a deterrent effect on marauders.

The Vincent Wallace affair called for a turnout of Lieutenant Waugh's men in full dress. The lieutenant did not bother with a lecture. He coldly stated that the felony of murder would be dealt with as swiftly as a court-martial could be set up, and curtly dismissed the regiment.

But more outrages did occur. Shortly after the murder of Vincent Wallace the renegades struck again, killing Daniel Farmer, burning the home of Bentley Gray, and torturing Mrs. S. J. Howell.

Another incident that raised the wrath of the townspeople occurred on May 19, 1864, when Waugh, now a lieutenant colonel of the Second Arkansas Regiment, USA, ordered the evacuation of Clarksville. Clarksville citizens accused him of attempting to burn the town due to the hatred generated by the murder of Vincent Wallace. Colonel Waugh did wreck the covered bridge and the courthouse, and he put a torch to the Methodist church and the supplies it contained, but he was acting under orders. "Fighting Joe" Shelby, the Confederate brigadier general, was calling northwest Arkansas his territory, and the federal command at Clarksville viewed with alarm the fast-moving forces of General Sterling Price.

Although the burning of the church angered the people, the sight of the food supplies being destroyed, meager though they were, produced bitterness. Food had become so scant that folks were digging the dirt from smokehouse floors. By refining the soil, a bit of dingy salt could be reclaimed—salt deposited from the drippings of meat in the pre-war years.

The evacuation of Clarksville proved to be only temporary. The federal troops soon returned, and remained until the end of the war. The hostility of the townspeople remained unabated.

The war's end brought little sunlight to Clarksville. If anything, the shadows of bleakness and poverty seemed to increase as the dread rule of the carpetbaggers fell upon the land. The tingling excitement of wartime was gone. The only solaces were the returning fathers, sons, brothers, sweethearts, and friends to improverished homes. Marauding bands of miscreants still terrorized the people. Inevitably, a slow readjustment began in Johnson County, but not for Sydney Wallace—fatherless, and maturing too rapidly in an era of unrest.

Tales of Jesse James and his Missouri freebooters became common topics of conversation. Newspapers, long since sated with publishing lists of war dead, welcomed a change of pace and considerable news space was devoted to the adventures of the James Gang. In Clarksville the outlaws were a favorite conversation piece for the loafers around the court square—the gang had been sighted a number of times in the county. And, there was a dandy rumor afloat that Jesse had come into town in the dead of night and left his baby son to be raised by some resident. It never came to light just who the glamorous youngster was.

Jesse James, of course, had the sympathy of the public with him for a long, long time. He was a hero in this bitter land, fighting back at hated enemies, fighting the Union-sympathizing lawmen, grasping railroads, carpetbaggers, and the uppity banks.

During these turbulent years Sid Wallace matured to

a fine physical specimen. Many young belles whispered among their friends when the striking young man rode by, and many limpid eyes were discreetly cast his way. "That Wallace boy," a handsome six-footer with broad shoulders and dark, wavy hair, was the secret love of most of the unspoken-for lasses. His dark blue eyes, almost sullen in expression, held a promise of wild romance, but the paternal hand of those days could bear heavily. Guest lists for social functions were carefully screened and members of feuding families, Republicans, and other types of undesirables were summarily scratched. Sid Wallace was a darkly angry man, and other men sensed it. With his good looks and family background he should have been the most popular young man at the Clarksville play-parties, but his enigmatic behavior left him with few invitations—and any that he received he rudely ignored.

People heard tell that Sid Wallace had sworn a mighty oath to avenge the murder of his father. In their hearts Johnson County residents cheered him, but no one knew how Sid could go about securing his revenge. However, the subject did create lively discussions. Sid was not a person to make idle threats, and he soon had the county humming with a story that rivaled Jesse James's derring-do.

As the story goes, Sid dressed as an enterprising drummer for a St. Louis mercantile company and rode away for the Kansas country. He cut a handsome figure with his expensive togs and big thoroughbred horse.

Sid arrived at a lonely farmhouse in Kansas just as dusk was falling. He knocked on the door and politely asked directions from the farmer and his wife. As Sid expected, the farmer insisted that the handsome stranger "light and eat," and spend the night. It was the custom of those days, and besides, no honest horseman traveled in that land at night, unless it was a matter of life and death.

During the informal hour after the evening meal and prior to the early bedtime, Sid "revealed" that he was "the son of

one of the soldiers stationed at Clarksville during the war."
He thus elicited the story from his host of "the shooting of
ol' Vint Wallace."

At daylight Sid was served a hot breakfast while one of
the farmer's sons prepared his horse for travel. The boy
brought the animal to the front gate of the farmhouse yard
and Sid came out of the house with the farmer. Mounting
the steed, Sid leaned in his saddle to shake hands with his
host. The farmer's family had gathered in the doorway to
watch their guest depart.

Shaking hands, Sid told the farmer, "I am Vint Wallace's
son." Jerking a huge Colt from under his coat, Sid shot the
man full in the face, and without a backward glance, spurred
his horse away.

3

"BLOODY CLARKSVILLE"

The initial legend of the avenging Sid Wallace, true or not, caught the fancy of the people of Johnson County. Staunch citizens of Clarksville, who would never look upon murder as the solution to any problem, were mild in their tongue-clucking. After all, young Wallace was fatherless and had matured from boyhood to his late teens nurturing a hatred instead of a worthwhile goal. Wild and headstrong, he had not found a place in the community struggle of erasing the scars of a bitter war.

In 1871 the construction of the Little Rock-Fort Smith Railroad was under way, and the iron rails were laid as far westward as the little town of Cabin Creek (Lamar), ninety-five miles out of Little Rock.

Clarksville became engrossed with all the possibilities of changes the new railroad would present. A number of farmers found it quite profitable to contract with the railroad to haul timbers for ties. Others hired out with their teams of horses or mules for "slip-shovel" work on track embankments and hillside cuts. Young bucks sought jobs to test their lithe muscles against the brawn of the professional track layers. The clinking of hard money was a melody long denied to the townspeople. The laughter of the coins could be heard when the railroad workers came to town on Saturday afternoons. And the activities of the Railroad

Company in securing the right-of-ways was a daily topic on the courthouse square.

The exploits of Sid Wallace were not to be placed secondary to the subject of the day—"the track," however.

Sid doubtlessly felt the heady surge that goes with "being noticed." He liked the feeling, and he was bent on having more of it.

Captain Dickey, a member of the railroad company, was traveling the Cabin Creek-Clarksville road with a companion in a buggy when he was halted by two masked riders. The horsemen materialized suddenly from the thick brush that bordered the road, and the railroad man instinctively hauled back on his reins. His companion, Dud Turner, pushed a tall hat off the bridge of his nose where the sudden stop of the vehicle had placed it, and he surveyed the mounted pair blocking the road.

The riders were well dressed, and they were astride splendid horses, but it was the gaudy bandannas that caught Turner's immediate attention. The horsemen were not only masked, but each wore a holstered revolver, and the arms were not the smaller belt type. They were huge army model Colts. The masks effectively hid the features of the riders but the two pairs of cold eyes showing above the bandannas were glittering with some unholy purpose.

Without speaking a word, and before the two men in the buggy could make a move, one of the masked riders snaked his Colt from its holster and fired. Turner felt Dickey jerk as the big bullet slammed into his head. A puff of blue gun smoke hung over the road as the horsemen plunged their mounts into the brush and vanished.

For a moment Turner was stupefied, but the rearing horse between the shafts of the buggy was causing the light vehicle to lurch and rock. Dazedly, he fumbled for the reins. Dickey's body toppled sideways and came to rest against his shoulder. Shoving the body back to an upright position, Turner shook the reins and bawled a command to the horse. The excited animal needed no coaxing to break into a full run.

Reaching over to the dashboard to seize the buggy whip from its socket, Turner shot a glance at the face of his dead friend. The unfortunate man had been shot neatly between the eyes. Turner lashed the horse furiously as his nerve began to desert him. He could cope with gun fire, but he wanted no companionship with a cadaver. The jouncing, lolling corpse in the seat beside him, with what appeared to be three eyes staring from a white, astonished face, had him completely demoralized before half the distance to Clarksville was covered.

Turner flailed the flying horse to a frenzy of speed, and the buggy was soon careening down East Hill. The crash of the madly running horse's hoofs, echoing from the hollow shell of the covered bridge, sounded an alert to the town. By the time the winded horse was hauled to a stop at the court square, men were running from all directions to ascertain what the racket was all about.

The dead man was lifted from the buggy and placed on a well-whittled wooden bench that graced the court square. Identification was quick, and the corpse was covered with a blanket. With his dead friend blanketed from his sight, Turner began to speak more coherently.

"Sid Wallace done the shooting," he stuttered.

The court square hummed with discussions, and the incident was soon spread across the county.

"Captain Dickey had something to do with the shooting of Vint Wallace," it was assumed throughout Johnson County.

With a suspect so plainly designated, local lawmen had little choice. Reluctantly, they saddled up and ventured out to the Wallace home. Nervously and with extreme politeness, they informed Sid that he was under arrest on suspicion of murder. To their astonishment, Sid proved docile, even amused at the charge. He readily saddled his favorite mount, a white mare, and calmly rode into town with his escort.

The lawmen elbowed the milling crowd on the court square to gain entrance to the courthouse. Sid was placed in an upstairs corner room of the gutted building. It was the only room still in sound condition, and it served the community as a jail.

Sid waited patiently as the door was locked and tested. As soon as the sounds of the lawmen's boots on the rickety wooden stairs had died away, he stepped over to the only window in the small room. The lock appeared old, and he exerted his lean strength, ripping the rusty mechanism loose from the wooden frame. With a quick jerk he raised the window and eased himself through the opening, dropping lightly to the roof of a shed that adjoined that side of the courthouse. From the shed he vaulted easily to the ground, and in broad daylight, he calmly strode away.

Arming himself at home with his two Colt revolvers and a double-barrel shotgun, Sid returned to his usual haunts.

Johnson County residents laughed. The law officers were appointed by the Republican Party, which in those demoralizing years of the Reconstruction Era, was anything but a popular regime. The minions of the law were thus held in even less esteem and were afforded only the bare necessities of civility. They dared not rearrest Sid.

Dud Turner fled to the Indian Territory for a few months.

Arkansas at this time was deep in the throes of the "Brooks-Baxter War." Brooks, a native of Iowa, was identified with the carpetbaggers, and Baxter, though a native of Arkansas, was a Republican and a Union follower during the late war. In a hotly fought race for the governor's chair in 1872, Baxter advocated the restoration of the franchise to ex-Confederate soldiers, and a strong law and order program. This was a program that smacked of the real needs of the people and he was elected. He quickly began putting some of his platform ingredients into action. It was a vivid era of politics for Arkansas. Among Governor Baxter's appointments was the naming of Elisha Meers to be the judge of the circuit that included Johnson County.

A native of Johnson County, but a Republican, Judge Meers was viewed with the usual distrust when he took his new job. A gifted man for the post, the judge soon made a name for himself. He adhered to the dictates of the law, but he handled the affairs of his office in an impartial manner. While never admired for his political affiliations, Judge Meers soon gained the respect of the community as an able and honest man.

The approaching railroad would mean a lot to Clarksville. The iron rails would bring the rest of the nation infinitely closer, and the familiar stagecoach, with its spirited span of horses, would soon be only a nostalgic memory. With an honest judge in town and the track layers already visiting on the streets, Clarksville began to feel the breath of a new life. Graying wooden store fronts, unpainted and neglected since the war years, were repaired and given bright coats of paint. Here and there, brand-new buildings were erected of cheerful, red bricks that were made up and fired not far from the court square.

Unlike the town, Sid Wallace had not changed. He and his brother, George, were often seen about town heavily armed. Hearing that Dud Turner had returned from Indian Territory and was back in town, the two brothers soon located him. They pounced on him and began administering a severe pistol-whipping without a show of mercy. Bystanders rushed in and prevented a killing.

Turner recovered in ten days, and the desire for revenge filled his aching head. He took up a post in an alley, just off Main Street, knowing that sooner or later the Wallace boys would pass the spot. Eventually, George Wallace came into sight. Turner called to him, and as Wallace wheeled around, Turner fired a blast from a shotgun. George staggered into a nearby general store and sat down heavily on a keg of nails. In a few minutes he died.

Sid Wallace was in Pat Flood's saloon, down near the covered bridge, when he heard the news of his brother's death. He made no comment, but walked silently out of the saloon as patrons up and down the bar eyed each other apprehensively.

Dud Turner was duly arrested, as he made no attempt to flee, but Judge Meers released him on a writ of habeas corpus. Then, Turner again vanished from the town. As the body of George lay in the Wallace home prior to the funeral, Sid excused himself and went away into the night. The next day the town buzzed with the news that a man named Davis had been called to his door during the late hours by a visitor. The visitor had opened fire and killed Davis.

The townfolks did not know what connection, if any, the shooting had to do with the Wallace affair. It was assumed though, that Sid was the gunman. This time, the town did not laugh. A dim view was taken of the shootings.

The local constabulary was in a quandary. They did not have a shred of evidence on which to charge Sid, and they were unsure of the status of Sid's public backing. Then too, Sid Wallace was not a man to approach casually with a warrant.

Finally, a break came for the lawmen. News reached town that Sid had accidentally shot himself in a foot while cleaning a gun. He was laid-up at his home. The lawmen figured that it was the best chance they were likely to get, and they surrounded the Wallace home.

However, instead of making the customary concerted rush, the lawmen hesitated. The horses pawed the ground as the riders conferred. Two problems existed. There were innocent people in the house, and the lawmen shuddered at the thought of reprisals that would follow if those people were injured or killed in an assault on the house. Secondly, they knew that Sid was perfectly aware of the cordon of armed men. No one would volunteer to go in the house and make the attempt to bring Sid out. It was an uneasy stalemate, and it was finally decided to tell Sid from a safe distance that he was under arrest.

"Sid, you are surrounded, and under arrest."

There was no answer to the loud call, and soon darkness began to close in.

Aunt Missouri Blackard, after the war's end, had elected to remain with the Wallace family. The weary watching posse saw the colored lady appear at the back door of the house with a large pail in her hand. Obviously, she was going after water. She left the doorway, looming large in the twilight with her billowing skirts, and walked slowly toward a nearby well. The posse relaxed.

When Aunt Missouri stopped at the well, a saddled horse that was tied to the pulley beam neighed softly. Suddenly, Sid popped out from underneath Aunt Missouri's voluminous skirts and leaped nimbly into the saddle. Before the astonished lawmen could gather their wits, Sid was only a drumming sound of distant hoofs in the darkness.

Clarksville again had a laugh, but it was not nearly as hearty as formerly.

Early one morning, August 20, 1873, "Doc" Ward, the town constable who had come to town during the war, was enjoying the sunup coolness. For years he had also enjoyed favor under the aegis of the carpetbaggers. On this particular morning he was settled in a chair on the wooden sidewalk in front of the McConnell Drug Store. Over in the court square the little frame courthouse presented a lonely picture, the glassless windows of the unused lower floor were staring blindly.

A sudden roar of a shotgun blast erupted from one of the vacant window squares, and the peace of the early morning was shattered.

Doc Ward slid slowly from his chair, sprawled on the wooden walk, and died in a widening pool of blood.

A crowd formed instantly, but no one saw the killer. For all the town knew, he was a member of the voluble, milling crowd. The officials were helpless, and no one came up with an idea of who the suspect could be. The town muttered, but no trace of the shotgunner was found.

A short while later Judge Meers walked slowly home, engrossed with the problems of his office and the murder of the town constable. At the end of Main Street he crossed Spadra Creek on the footwalk of the covered bridge, appreciating the cool interior. Emerging in the humid heat of the late afternoon, he slowly walked up East Hill. He turned to the right, and took his customary short cut across a small field. After crossing the field he stooped to climb through a fence of loose wires. Just as he straightened on the other side of the fence the boom of a shotgun blast knocked him from his feet.

Drawn by the gunshot, a small crowd quickly gathered. Judge Meers's long black coat, the badge of his office that he wore despite the summer heat, was stained with dust and bright red blood. He was tenderly carried to the home of School Commissioner Littlebury Robinson, the nearest house, and placed on a bed. Bleeding profusely from a gaping wound, Judge Meers died within the hour.

Absent from his home on both occasions, Sid Wallace was blamed for the murders of Doc Ward and Judge Meers. Weary of the acrid odor of gun smoke, Clarksville began demanding a cleanup. Sid's absence served to strengthen his status as prime suspect, and his public backing was melting away.

Littlebury Robinson's sister was en route from Little Rock to Clarksville on the now seldom used stagecoach, and a lone horseman passed. She recognized Sid Wallace, and when the coach arrived at the town of Conway, notified the authorities.

Sheriff Stoudt and City Marshal Polk Alnut trailed Sid to a ford on Point Remove Creek. As Sid was urging his horse across the stream the officers got the drop on him and

relieved him of his firearms. The lawmen then brought Sid
to Clarksville.

Sid was indicted for the murders of Captain Dickey,
Doc Ward, and Judge Meers. He was not without friends,
however. Many people, still tender from the roughshod
methods of the law at the height of the carpetbagger
regime, did not want a man tried for murder when there
was not sufficient proof that he was guilty. Dud Turner
had long ago disappeared. Strong rumors had it that Sid
would not stand trial.

Consequently, a furor was created when the prosecution
announced that a Tom Paine would testify that he saw
Sid Wallace kill Doc Ward. Most folks were reasonably
sure that Sid was the guilty party, but they had no stomach
or patience for attempts to "railroad" him. With the alleged
eyewitness, the state elected to try Sid for the murder of
Ward.

The trial did not start smoothly, for Tom Paine disappeared. Some folks muttered that the Wallace clan had
paid Tom to leave. Others said that they couldn't much
blame ol' Tom for leaving, figuring that the man was living
on borrowed time after the announcement of the prosecution.

However, someone reported Paine's whereabouts. He was
holed up in the Indian Territory. Armed with a subpoena,
deputy U.S. marshals, working in the Western District of
Arkansas, obligingly returned the key witness to Clarksville.

Paine was close-mouthed and bitter.

Just before the trial began Paine was accosted on the
street by a man named Clark. No one overheard the exchange of words. Clark made a fast draw, but his pistol
failed to discharge. Paine drew his own weapon and
wounded Clark, who was then jailed on a charge of attempted murder.

The town simmered with the new developments, but no
solution was publicly heard as to the riddle of Clark's

position in the affair. The two principals refused to discuss the matter, and the handsome Sid only smiled mysteriously in his cell, increasing the gossip generally.

The trial of Sid Wallace was set for November 11, 1873, and Clarksville was ready for action, in more ways than one. The rumors swelled apace—Sid Wallace would not stand trial, he was going to be sprung! Newspapers across the state gave the impending Wallace trial a big play, and the town was soon dubbed "Bloody Clarksville."

Governor Baxter went into action. He ordered a special militia created, and he sent guns to arm it.

"Talk of a jail break must cease," the governor thundered.

Perhaps as a result of the armed militia, Sid's trial moved quickly, and no more shootings occurred. The testimony of the perspiring Tom Paine and the trumpeting charge of the prosecutor brought a quick verdict of guilty. Sid was sentenced to be hung December 23, 1873, and he was placed in the "new" county jail, situated on the third floor of the huge brick Hershey building just to the northeast of the court square. Clarksville had decided that a durable calaboose was in order.

On November 25, at 4 P.M., Tom and Matt, younger brothers of Sid Wallace, obtained permission to visit their jailed brother. The three young men chatted on ordinary subjects until Sid saw that the two armed guards were relaxing their vigil. In a flash he grabbed a shotgun out of the hands of one of them and quickly disarmed the other. He then forced the terrified guards to go down the stairs.

Presently, the Wallace boys, and the bandaged Clark in an adjacent cell, heard the electric cry on the street below:

"The Wallaces have captured the jail!"

Sid Wallace glared through the jail bars of a window. The third floor view from the Hershey building afforded Sid a section of Main Street. It was only a little after 4 o'clock, and the street should have been dotted with people and wagon traffic. The street was bare.

The town was not deserted, though. Hoarse shouts could be heard, and boots were drumming on the wooden sidewalks somewhere beyond Sid's view. A thin beading of perspiration glistened on Sid's forehead. Cursing softly to himself, he pulled a large bandanna from his hip pocket and wiped his face. The chill of a November day crept in the opened window behind the bars, but Sid ignored it.

Matt and Tom Wallace were silent, eying their brother, determined to back him in any move he decided to make. Clark was staring, big-eyed, at Sid, uncertain as to the direction Wallace's wrath would be aimed. Clark was perspiring freely.

"Sid," Matt began—but he did not get a chance to finish his remark. Sid suddenly came erect at his window post. He shoved the bandanna back into his hip pocket and cradled his cheek to the butt of the shotgun. Sid's indecision vanished, for here was something he could cope with.

Tom Paine, pistol in hand, stepped out of a doorway in a building next to the Hershey structure. By tilting the barrels of his gun at a sharp angle, Sid managed to get a bead. With the boom of the shotgun Paine pitched headlong into the street, dead before he plowed into the dust.

There were excited cries below, and three men bravely rushed into view. Hastily seizing Paine's body, they dragged it from sight of the jail window. Sid calmly inspected his piece to see if another charge remained.

"Ol' Tom won't do any more lying," he observed.

Matt and Tom made no comment, but their worried faces indicated they knew what had transpired. Clark's damp face was waxy. He appeared to be on the verge of vomiting.

Suddenly, the bark of a pistol from the street below sent a leaden bullet clanging against the bars of the window. The Wallace boys instinctively ducked, and Sid risked a hasty glance out of the window. The man in the street was

D. Winders, and he evidently had just emerged from a saloon a few doors away. Winders was unsteadily taking aim for a second shot, using both hands in the attempt. Sid ducked.

The shot roared, but the bullet hit the brick wall and caromed off into the distance, buzzing angrily.

Sid bellowed, "Get away, you damned fool, I don't want to shoot you!"

Winders let out a jovial whoop, and fired again. This time his bullet zipped neatly through the window and thudded against the far wall of the jail room. Clark let out a whimper of terror and crept under his bunk.

With the echoes of the shot, Sid raised up and thrust the barrels of his gun through the bars. He blasted Winders' legs with buckshot.

Winders dropped to his knees with a yelp, but he quickly crawled out of sight, considerably sobered.

Sid heard the sound of heavy footsteps inside the building. Winder's diversion had permitted the sheriff and his deputies to gain the downstairs portion of the structure. Sid ground out a curse.

A leather-lunged voice blared up the stair well:

"Wallace, we got a keg of powder and a fuse. We have busted open a back door so we can get out. If you don't throw them guns outen the winder right now, we're lightin' the fuse!"

From underneath Clark's bunk came a desperate screech: "Give 'em the damned guns!"

Tossing the empty shotgun to his bewildered brothers, Sid made motions for them to reload it with powder and shot from a supply on the guard's desk. Then he called down the stair well.

"Let my two brothers come down, and I'll talk about it."

"Wallace," came the answer, "you got just one minute."

Sid cursed, but he could tell by the rough voices that the lawmen were not bluffing, and he made a characteristic

quick decision. Taking the loaded shotgun, he cocked back
the hammers and leaned it against the wall. He then picked
up a Winchester and cocked it. From his waistband he
drew out a Colt six gun. He knew that the two guards had
informed the lawmen as to the exact number of firearms in
his possession. He eared back the big hammer of the Colt
and picked up the two long guns. He stepped to the open
window and thrust the artillery through the bars. The guns
fell to the street with a clatter, but only the shotgun discharged. A cluster of lead balls flew from the unmanned
gun, and far down the street a man named Taylor was
struck in the heel.

Sid strode quickly to the head of the stair and called
down:

"All right, you bastards, you can come up now."

The lawmen advanced cautiously up the stairs with
cocked guns ready. Matt and Tom Wallace were arrested
and sent to the jail at Van Buren, Arkansas, to await trial
on a charge of aiding in the killing of Tom Paine. Sid was
hustled off to the penitentiary at Little Rock, escorted, at
Governor Baxter's suggestion, by a hastily recruited group
of armed Clarksville citizens.

4

THE AEGIS OF BUD MCCONNELL

Sid Wallace appeared to have changed considerably when he reached the penitentiary in Little Rock. He no longer was in doubt as to whether "the people" were still behind him. He became reckless where he had formerly displayed calculated daring. One day, he exerted his best personal charm until he had the guard unwary, whereupon he snatched a pistol.

A group of Little Rock citizens happened to be touring the penitentiary facilities that day, and they chanced upon the tableau—a good-looking young man with a cocked revolver in his fist, glaring through the bars of a locked cell at a frightened guard.

It was a cool-headed group of Little Rockians. They sized up the situation, and informed Sid of a fact that he had overlooked, the guard did not have the key to the cell. Cell keys were kept in the office of the head jailer, up in the front part of the jail building.

Even if Sid killed six people with all the loads in the gun, he would still be in a locked cell, the citizens argued.

Sid lowered the revolver. He rather admired the pluck of the visitors. With a laugh, he uncocked the gun and passed it through the bars to the relieved guard. The guard was levied a stiff fine for his laxity.

The newspapers found Sid to be excellent copy, and the references to "Bloody Clarksville" appeared again and again. Clarksville boiled. The unwanted publicity irked the people nearly as much as the community shootings, and Sid Wallace became a famous Arkansas figure.

Wallace won an appeal to the Supreme Court, but the decision went against him, and he was sentenced to hang March 14, 1874.

As the date for Sid's hanging neared, the rumors that seemed to always accompany the Wallace case began to fly thick and fast. One juicy rumor even had Sid involved with a romance.

It seems that an official of the state penitentiary had a stunningly beautiful but spoiled daughter. Little Rock was reviving a social phase that was famous before the war, the Cotton Cotillion. The mammoth social event was the high-water mark in the lives of Little Rock debutantes. The willful daughter of the penitentiary official prevailed upon her doting father to secure the escort service of that "divinely handsome prisoner from Clarksville." It was so arranged, and romantically minded gossipers babbled about the "dashing appearance" of Sid Wallace in formal dress as he escorted the breath-taking beauty to the glittering ball. The story went on to a theatrical finale. The girl was completely won by the charming Sid, as handsome as a stage idol and as glamorous as Jesse James. When she pleaded with her father to spirit Sid away, so she could marry him in a far distant locale, the father came to his senses. The grim clanging of the iron cell door on Sid was the echo of his emphatic refusal.

Few Clarksville citizens doubted the rumors of Sid's social life in Little Rock. As one fellow put it, during a discussion on the court square of "the Wallace story":

"Hell, that good-looking devil can charm the whiskers offen a cat!"

The emergency militia that had been created to escort Sid to the penitentiary at Little Rock had been led by E. T. "Bud" McConnell, a stocky young man with a fierce black mustache and a jutting jaw. A veteran of the late war, he had joined a company organized by his brother Will, and had fought through the war years for the Confederacy. As with his legions of gray-clad comrades, McConnell had felt the salty sting of defeat when the news of Appomattox reached them in the field.

But it was the return home that had shriveled Bud McConnell's soul. He had left a prosperous and pleasant home town, only to return to a scene of rude poverty and political sickness. A fiery man, McConnell wasted no time on self-pity. He began farming, and despite poor markets he soon had enough capital to invest in more land. He took over the management of a drugstore his father had founded before the war, and he brought that establishment out of the postwar doldrums. Following a pattern, that three quarters of a century later would be commonplace with drugstores, he stocked his concern with myriad goods: drugs and medicines, chemicals, perfumery, soaps, combs and brushes, trusses, supports and shoulder braces, fancy and toilet articles, books and stationery, oils, varnishes and dyestuffs, and patent medicines.

Without pausing to survey his progress, McConnell, with George Jamison as a partner, set up a job printing shop and established the Clarksville *Enterprise,* a weekly newspaper that, by its title, reflected his ideas of dragging the town from the postwar decadence to a place in the sun.

Bud McConnell liked the newspaper profession, he could "reach" people, and he was not velvet-gloved in editorially watch-dogging the community interests. Upon learning that two architects—drawing up separate plans for a new courthouse—had each been paid a fee, the *Enterprise* demanded a full explanation. The presence of a vigorous newspaper in the county was infinitely a boon, but McConnell often chewed his cheroot in helpless anger as he was forced to print "the news." The repetitious phrase of "Bloody Clarksville" galled him to the point that he decided to do something about it.

Stories of Sid's romance did not perturb Bud McConnell. He refused to honor the rumors in print, but the growing reports that "Sid Wallace would never stand on the trap door of a gallows" alerted him. He had no illusions about the complexity of the Wallace case.

The "Wallace rumors" reached a climax when a story was circulated that an attempt would be made to free Sid when he was placed aboard a train for his shackled journey to Clarksville for hanging. An unknown group would way-lay the train somewhere between Little Rock and Clarksville, and Deputy Sheriff E. A. Kline, who had already departed for the capital city to serve as an armed escort, would be offered $2000 to permit Sid's escape. The rumor also had it that in the event Kline should prove stubborn, he would be gunned down, and Sid would be removed from the train anyhow.

Bud McConnell exploded. "Not by a damned sight!" he roared. He went into action immediately.

The Little Rock-Fort Smith Railroad had now been completed as far west as Clarksville. It was early Sunday morning, and there would be no trains running on the Sabbath. The Little Rock train had arrived the day before, and the crew was asleep at a boardinghouse down by the tracks. Early Monday morning they would turn their train on the temporary turntable and leave for the capital city.

Bud McConnell mentally made a list of fourteen dependable citizens. With the aid of the first man aroused, he quickly had them assembled. He laid out his plan of action:

"As all of you know, or have heard, someone is going to jump the train out of Little Rock Tuesday, and Sid Wallace may get loose. Deputy Sheriff Kline is down there now. We'll take this train and join him, and we'll bring Sid back."

Completing his briefing, Bud led his posse to the trainmen's boardinghouse. He clumped up a flight of stairs to a bedroom and awakened Conductor T. Hartman. The conductor, hair tousled and pants pulled hastily over sockless feet, accompanied McConnell downstairs. He was dumbfounded at the audacity of the Clarksville men as he listened to their request. Shaking his head a few times, he became angered.

"Can't run my train off schedule. The telegraph is out of whack, won't be fixed until tomorrow, and there is no way of notifying Little Rock. On Sundays Superintendent Beaumont usually authorizes a short-run repair train, and I can't risk a collision."

"Look, mister," the impatient McConnell snapped, his flinty eyes boring into Hartman's face, "you don't know about this town or the trouble that has happened and the trouble that is brewing. This is a matter of life and death."

"Well," said the conductor uneasily, "I'll give the order for the run if you can get the engineer to operate the locomotive."

Hartman was certain that the engineer would refuse to be ordered, especially where his beloved engine was concerned.

McConnell bellowed for the engineer and his fireman to come down into the street. The engineer, a hulking man, soon joined the group, and in a couple of minutes the fireman appeared. They listened to the request to "borrow" the train, and the engineer promptly refused.

"Well now, by damn," snarled the big trainman, "there ain't no townsite jasper going to tell me when to run my engine!"

The huge figure of the engineer towered over the stocky McConnell. Bud's heavy jaw jutted forward, and his thick mustache raised. He jerked a six gun from underneath his coat.

"Let's get up steam," he barked.

In jigtime the fireman was industriously heaving chunks of wood into the boiler of the diamond-stack locomotive.

Soon he signaled that the necessary steam pressure was showing on the gauge. The Clarksville posse followed the conductor aboard.

The engineer was glumly at work with a big oil can near the huge drivers of the locomotive.

"—run the engine in a ditch and kill the whole damn bunch—that's what I'll do—"

The engineer was muttering direly to himself, and Bud McConnell overheard him. Motioning to the angry trainman to mount the cab of the engine, McConnell swung up the ladder after him, six-shooter in hand.

"We'll have a fast, safe run to Little Rock," he announced.

The little train chuffed its way, without incident, to Argenta (North Little Rock), the terminus. A group of astounded train officials rushed over to the station to ascertain why their rolling stock was one hundred miles and twenty-four hours off schedule.

The superintendent "swore like a pirate."

Bud McConnell and his posse walked away while the train crew was explaining the presence of the train to their bosses. Out of sight of the little depot, Bud paused.

"You men be here early in the morning—we'll take the regular train back. I'm going on into Little Rock and in the morning Kline and I will have Sid here."

Leaving his friends, McConnell searched for a hack to hire. Soon, he was across the Arkansas River and in the city of Little Rock.

After an early breakfast, Bud arrived at the state penitentiary. He made his way to the row of cells, and located one that had a cluster of men at its door. Greeting the surprised Kline, McConnell was introduced to the head jailer and the warden. The warden listened to McConnell's plan to escort Sid as Bud explained to Kline:

"Story has it in Clarksville that a bunch of men will bushwhack you on your way there. I've got fourteen men waiting at Argenta that says they won't."

Kline nodded, glad of the reinforcement, and the warden offered the services of a guard as far as Argenta.

"No, thanks," answered the stocky McConnell, "Kline and I can handle it."

"Well," said the Warden, "if you boys have to catch a train, we'll get busy. Kline, if you'll come to my office and sign the release slip, we'll hand over the prisoner."

While waiting for the return of Kline, McConnell peered through the bars of the cell. He watched the tall young prisoner with interest. Sid Wallace appeared to be tense, but he was neither frightened nor cocky.

"We aim to have a quiet, peaceful trip to Clarksville," McConnell said, softly.

Two pairs of hard eyes stared in an exchange of appraisal, but Sid only nodded slowly. McConnell wondered if he even knew of the planned attempt to free him.

Kline returned with a pair of guards, and Sid's cell door was quickly unlocked. Kline placed a pair of heavy mana-cles on Wallace's wrists, and the penitentiary men re-linquished the prisoner. Bud's hired hack was waiting, and the trio made a quick trip to Argenta. The train was at the station and a baggage crew was industriously loading the baggage car. The Clarksville posse was assembled on the platform.

McConnell jumped from the hack and hauled out his big watch.

"Three minutes to go," he observed, and then he waved to his posse.

"We'll take the last car, men. Split up—half of you take the back part, the rest of you take the front seats. Let's go."

McConnell and Kline hustled their prisoner aboard and the posse was arranged so that Sid was completely sur-rounded.

With the task completed, McConnell sat down in one of the red mohair-covered seats and struck a match on the sole of his boot. He applied the flame to a black cheroot and blew smoke rather absent-mindedly toward the ceiling of the coach. Something seemed amiss. Bud rubbed his chin thoughtfully. He had fully expected a force of railroad men to attempt blocking the posse on the return trip.

The locomotive gave a warning shriek with its whistle, and McConnell snapped his fingers—that was it. Things were just too quiet. He flung his cheroot into a brass cuspidor and bounced out of the seat.

"Take charge here, Kline," he called as he ran down the aisle, "I'm riding that engine back to Clarksville."

Bud leaped from the vestibule of the coach to the station platform just as the locomotive belched into action. His sudden suspicion was correct; the trainmen had uncoupled the coach containing the Clarksville men.

Pulling his Stetson firmly in place, Bud sprinted down the platform, overhauling the slowly moving train and climbing aboard the locomotive. The engineer stared, wide-eyed, into the muzzle of the big Colt in McConnell's fist. The bore of the weapon was more cavernous to the startled engineer than the yawning red pit of the engine's firebox.

"Back her up," McConnell grated.

The engineer hastily closed his throttle and set the Johnson bar. In a few moments time a soft jar indicated contact with the abandoned coach. Bud leaned from the cab window and shot a quick glance rearward. One of his possemen was waving, indicating the coupling pin was in place.

"Open her up," snapped McConnell, his cold eyes riveted on the engineer. The fireman energetically bent to his task of feeding cordwood to the hungry firebox.

The huge stack of the locomotive erupted in a flurry of brilliant sparks, and a billowing ball of wood smoke raced skyward as the big drivers blurred with quick frenzy. The wild thunder of the exhaust suddenly died as the drivers found a hold on the rails, and the train lurched into motion.

The exhaust stack began sounding a rapidly increasing tempo of barks.

Superintendent Beaumont and several of his staff were brought swarming out of the station by the unorthodox commotion of the locomotive, but they were too late. The train was moving faster than a man could run. The two brass lamps on the back of the rear coach—one with a red lens and the other green—twinkled impishly in the cheerful glow of the early morning sun—like the eyes of a happy heathen idol.

The superintendent shook his fist and shouted salty phrases, but no one on the train could hear him.

Bud watched the track carefully from his swaying perch in the locomotive cab, but nothing out of the ordinary caught his keen eyes. He permitted the engineer to make the routine stops at towns along the track, but passengers boarding the train were waved away from the last coach by the nervous Kline.

"This coach is reserved," he would gruffly announce, and as his shiny badge and holstered six-shooter were in plain sight, none argued the point.

The train eventually chuffed into Clarksville and was greeted by a crowd considerably larger than the customary group of train-greeters. Sid was quickly conveyed to his cell in the hulking Hershey building. His manacles were not removed from his wrists, and an extra pair of guards was posted.

Confined with maximum security, Sid Wallace had little reason to expect a boon. His catlike wariness slowly diminished. He could hear the busy pounding of carpenters down the street, and he knew they were erecting a stout scaffold.

Clarksville had finally raised enough money to erect a new courthouse. The old wrecked hull of the frame structure had been removed, and already the brown brick walls of the new building were up on the court square. The interior

was not yet finished, and the small upstairs room, reserved
for the purpose, did not have the planned trap door in
place—the "indoors gallows" was incomplete. Consequently,
temporary measures were necessary. Carpenters soon completed a rough but workable gallows on the grounds of the
court square—on the spot Sid Wallace would have had to
stand in order to shoot Doc Ward.

Bud McConnell, contrary to Sid's sense of doom, knew
that a simple fact, and strategy, existed. The transition of
Wallace from his cell to the scaffold would offer an ideal
situation to the mysterious "friends" of the condemned man.
It would be possible for a force of hard-riding men to
swoop down on the local law the moment Sid was led from
his cell.

April 13, 1874, a special guard was assembled with Bud
McConnell as captain. McConnell had selected his men and
he had worked with them for hours on a pattern of action
in the event trouble erupted on hanging day.

"Hanging day" drew a tremendous crowd into town, but
there was little evidence of a holiday mood. Folks in general
seemed to think that the bloody era was about to end. It
was not a time for gay celebrating, instead it would be
more appropriate to mark the end of bloodshed with devout
thankfulness. It was obvious that Bud McConnell did not
believe the shooting era was past. He knew for a certainty
that the only reason Sid Wallace was not freed on the
return trip from Little Rock was the fact that a heavily
armed guard was present. Bud was equally certain that his
"hanging day army" was the only guarantee the town had
for an orderly hanging.

Bud passed out the arms that Governor Baxter had
supplied for the special militia, and he stationed a number
of men along Main Street for the short distance from the
Hershey building to the corner of the court square where
the gallows was squatting.

The guards went to work maintaining an open avenue

for the procession that was soon to commence. The milling crowd grew in density as the hanging hour neared, and a pall of quietness descended.

Deputy Sheriffs Littlepage, and Wilson were on duty at the entrance to the Hershey building. Deputy Sheriff Kline had escorted a contingent of armed men and "civilians" up the stairs to the cell room. In the group were Sid's mother, his brother Will, the Reverend I. N. Burrow of the Methodist church, and presiding Elder F. M. Paine. Also in the group was a heavily veiled young lady, and the crowd contented itself with conjecturing if the girl was the daughter of the jail official at Little Rock. However, this tidbit of romance had little effect on the funereal essence of the impending drama.

Knowing that the moment was at hand, all the merchants locked up their stores and joined the crowds. Upstairs, Kline made his preparations to bring Sid out. Following the family visit, a short prayer service was held, and Sid's relatives were escorted to another room. Kline set to work on the manacles that were clamped on Sid's wrists. The ancient cuffs did not receive the key smoothly, and Kline's sweaty hands impeded his nervous efforts. He could not help but admire Sid's calm and rather pleasant composure. Sid's dark blue eyes, however, reflected his sorrow of parting with his family.

Kline escorted Sid down the stairs to the doorway. Bud McConnell and two guards immediately conducted the law-man and prisoner to the street where a hack stood. A back seat had been removed from the vehicle, and Sid's coffin had been placed aboard. Without a glance at the somber box, Sid climbed into the front seat as Kline hurried around to the opposite side and got in. Snatching up the reins, Kline clucked the horse into a slow walk along the open lane through the packed crowd. McConnell and his two guards walked behind the hack, sweeping the rows of faces on either side with keen glances.

As the hack neared the northwest corner of the court square the crowds from both sides of the street fell in behind the hack like the churning wake of an ocean vessel. Ahead, the guards maintained an open avenue until the hack reached the gallows. In a moment the armed men had deserted the street and completely surrounded the squat rigging of raw yellow lumber.

Kline dismounted from the hack and Sid slid over and leaped out behind him. Kline took Sid's arm and led him up the shallow steps to the platform of the gallows. The Reverend Burrow and Elder Paine followed, while Kline busied himself tying Sid's hands behind his back. A group of out-of-town newspaper reporters was permitted to stand at the foot of the steps, and they gazed curiously up at the man who was about to die.

Sid Wallace was easily the most composed man on the platform. In response to Kline's query for any last remarks, Sid took a step forward, and addressed the silent throng.

"Gentlemen," he said, in a firm and clear voice, "I expect you came here expecting to hear me make confessions. I have no confessions to make to men, I make my confessions to God. I die in defense of myself and friends, and I only wish I had a half dozen lives to give the same way!"

The silence was so complete that the nervous Kline could hear the rapid scratching of the pencils of the newsmen as they jotted down Sid's last remarks. Kline took Sid's arm and asked him to step back a pace, to "center" on the trap door. Kline then placed the noose around Sid's neck.

The Reverend Burrow, his face showing considerable emotion, leaned forward and whispered:

"Son, die with a prayer on your lips."

Sid nodded.

"Lord, remember me when thou comest into thy Kingdom."

Kline took a deep breath and jerked the lever, and a gasp soughed up from the crowd as the trap snapped open.

Soon, Drs. Mitchell, Connelley, and Maffit broke the silence by snapping shut their pocket watches in unison. They mounted the platform and examined the body. They pronounced Sid Wallace dead with solemn nods of their heads in unison. The body was placed in the coffin and delivered to the Wallace home.

As the hack bearing the remains of Sid Wallace rumbled through the covered bridge, the packed crowd slowly milled until it was transformed into many little groups to discuss the day's events. The after-image of the striking figure of Sid Wallace standing resolutely on the gallows platform was seared on the memories of hundreds of people. The women, whose numbers almost equaled the men in the crowd, wondered how such a good-looking man could be guilty of all the crimes laid at his feet, and the men on the court square all admired Wallace's guts.

Bud McConnell heaved a sigh and formally dismissed his guard force. He strolled down the crowded wooden sidewalk to his newspaper office, slapping a large manila envelope against his thigh in rhythm with his stride. The railroad company had sent him a bill for $125, the charges for the use of the train he had commandeered. Bud had carefully packaged a sheaf of Johnson County script money —one hundred and twenty-five dollars' worth—in a manila envelope and mailed it to the company. The envelope had come back to him that morning on the Little Rock train. The railroad company had discovered that Johnson County script was worth only fifteen cents on the dollar.

Bud's agate eyes twinkled. His smile was soon to leave his face, however, for the Wallace affair was not yet finished.

A few days after the hanging, Deputy Sheriff Kline was walking uptown from the new railroad depot. Arriving at Main Street he turned right, and as he passed an alley a charge of buckshot erupted noisily, and the lawman was rocked to his knees. He jerked out his six gun and crawled to the alley entrance. He groaned; no one was in sight. Racing to the scene, citizens helped the angry lawman to his feet. He was not seriously wounded.

A day or so later Kline was recuperating in his room at the Woolem Hotel on west Main Street. His window offered a view of the street, and his bed had been placed so that he could while away the time watching passers-by.

Sid Wallace's brother Will, and a cousin, Robert Wallace, jogged slowly by on horses, and they saw the reclining Kline peering from his window. They pointed with their fingers, and laughed derisively, and rode on. Trotting their horses the length of Main Street, they clattered through the covered bridge and rode up East Hill. Topping the hill the horses slowed to a walk, and suddenly the hard jar of two shotgun blasts boomed. Both riders were knocked out of their saddles, but Will was not badly injured. Robert was bleeding excessively and onlookers, attracted by the noise of the unseen shotguns, carried him into the Little- bury Robinson home. In a few minutes Robert Wallace died on the same bed where Judge Meers had breathed his last.

Robert had been riding Sid's spirited white horse. The frightened animal bolted when the weight of the rider sud- denly left the saddle. In a wild, headlong run the horse raced to the Wallace home. As it came up to the front gate, it fell dead.

Bud McConnell roared as he reviewed the details of the shootings in his own newspaper. Was some sort of lengthy, bloody vendetta in the making? Bud didn't know, but he figured that a plan of action was needed. He wadded up a proof sheet and flung it to the floor of his littered print shop.

"What we need," he growled, "is a tough, efficient body of lawmen."

It was obvious that the mere hanging of one lawbreaker could not stop a wave of lawlessness. Bud seated himself at his battered desk and reached for a well-chewed pen. He thought about John N. Sarber, an astute politician of Clarksville who had received an appointment as United States Marshal of the Western District of Arkansas.

"He's got a hanging coming up in August," McConnell muttered, "and I'll wager it won't stop all that killing going on in the Indian Territory."

McConnell began scribbling rapidly:

"As to this business of stopping murders and shootings, you've got to have the right kind of lawmen, the right kind of a Judge, and then the laws that we have can get the job done."

The beginning of a series of articles was flowing from McConnell's pen, and the law-enforcement system was destined for a change.

5

THE INDIAN TERRITORY

Bud McConnell was correct. Marshal John N. Sarber of the Federal Court at Fort Smith, Arkansas, did have a hanging on the books. And he would have been the first man to endorse McConnell's assertion that "a hanging won't necessarily put an end to killings."

Marshal Sarber, however, was preparing to become a "civilian" again. He would not be around to supervise the scheduled hanging, for the resignation of Judge Storey in that month of June 1874 had put Sarber out of office. Without regrets, Sarber was packing to return to his home in Clarksville. Not quite a year had passed since the marshal had supervised his first hanging, and he could now voice the opinion of an authority on the subject; hangings had not deterred the increasing number of murders in the vast Indian Territory jurisdiction of the court. In fact, there were more warrants for capital crime perpetrators accumulated in the marshal's office than there had been the day he took the post.

John Newton Sarber was not a newcomer to the scene of savage murder. A native of Pittsburgh, Pennsylvania, he had been in Kansas when the war broke out. He enlisted in a Kansas Federal Cavalry unit and for a portion of the war had been stationed in occupied Clarksville, serving as a scout for Colonel Cloud. He took a liking to the bedraggled town and remained when the war ended. Though a Yankee,

he was finally accepted by the citizens, for the ex-Fed
soldier possessed a great amount of dignity and ambition.
He began a study of law, and in 1867 he married Susan
Rose, a striking beauty who was the daughter of Moreau
Rose, one of the original settlers of Clarksville.

As a Republican, Sarber's status was much the same as
Judge Elisha Meers, he did not belong to the "right" party.
However, the quality of his character transcended his affilia-
tion with the hated political regime and he easily won a
seat in the Arkansas legislature, serving in the 16th, 17th,
and 18th sessions as senator from Johnson County. In
1872, he presented a bill that created a new county. At
first named Sarber, the new county was later changed to
bear the name of Logan, to honor a pioneer settler, James
Logan. Fate seemed determined to thwart John Sarber's
bid for posterity. A small post office in a mountain community north of Clarksville was named in his honor. Somehow, the spelling was garbled, and the little post office
went on the records as "Garber," and that is the name of
the community to this day.

Sarber worked diligently to build a law practice, but he
always allowed time for political activities. He served on
the Board of Trustees of the Arkansas Industrial College of
Fort Smith. He was a member of the committee that
selected a new site for the school, moving it from Fort
Smith to Fayetteville.

Appointed Marshal of the Western District of Arkansas,
Sarber tackled the job at Fort Smith with his usual vigor.
However, he soon became appalled at the fearful task con-
fronting lawmen in the Indian Territory. The types and
rate of reported crimes was a staggering factor, and the
seat of Federal law was in a shameful condition.

The Indian Territory was a stepchild born of the famed
1803 Louisiana Purchase, which had wedded the fledgling
United States to a gigantic western acreage. An act of
Congress created the new home for the Cherokee, Choctaw,

Seminole, Creek, and Chickasaw Indian Tribes then dwelling in southern states east of the surging Mississippi River. The "Great Removals" of these, the "Five Civilized Tribes," were practically completed by the early 1870s. The old tribal governments worked well in governing the new "Nations," but, these governments had no provisions for prosecuting a white man who was wanted for a felony in the "States." Outlaws, quick to recognize this man-made legal quirk and the natural frontier fastness of the Territory as a haven, mingled with the incoming settlers. Neither genre had legal right of entry. The only threat to the outlaw and the only recourse for the settlers were thinly spread deputy U.S. marshals who were headquartered at Fort Smith, Arkansas. There was no precedent in United States history for this condition, and the latent crime breeding factors were not long in spawning the "land of the six-shooter."

It was on the fifteenth of August, 1873, that Sarber's now famous first hanging had taken place. It was an event that made a legend in an area grown accustomed to gruesome murder. Newspaper accounts of the event could have passed for Ned Buntline's prose in the dime novels of the era.

And of course, Marshal John Sarber would retain a vivid memory of the bizarre hanging for the rest of his days. On that fateful August day he was soberly surveying the huge gallows. A brassy sun high above was baking the grounds surrounding the United States Court buildings in Fort Smith. The big gallows, designed to launch six men simultaneously into eternity, was only two years old. The timbers of the structure were not fully grayed by the weather, and the mechanism had been maintained in good adjustment. The rig had not been put to the task for which it had been built, but a baptism was near at hand.

Marshal John Sarber extracted a crisp linen kerchief from a pocket of his black vest. With precise motions, the thirty-six-year-old lawman mopped his streaming face, which was devoid of the tan and wind burn common to men of his profession. A starched white shirt, accentuated by a jet black string tie, reflected the brilliant sunlight and matched the paleness of his finely molded features. In contrast, a short-clipped beard of dark brown color adorned the lower portion of his face.

A hanging demanded that many little chores be accomplished before the noose was utilized. Marshal Sarber mounted the thirteen steps that led to the platform of the gallows. Despite the terrific heat of the day his erect, military bearing and immaculate dress were not altered by the summer discomfort. Though he was a rather short man of medium build, the broad, squared shoulders of the marshal presented an excellent picture of authority as he stepped out onto the platform. The eyes of an enormous crowd that ringed the structure of death were fixed on the lawman. The polished silver badge of Sarber's office stood out in stark contrast to the black of his vest. At his side was an Army Model percussion Colt revolver. The big weapon was encased in a satiny black finish leather holster that was suspended by a wide leather belt of the same color around the lawman's slender waist.

The marshal glanced at the huge throng that filled the court grounds. As he adjusted his severely blocked black Stetson to shade a pair of keenly intelligent blue eyes, he noticed with some amazement that quite a number of women and children were in the audience. Vaguely angered, he wheeled and turned his attention to the mechanics of the gallows.

Grasping the iron actuating lever, Sarber braced himself and gave a powerful pull. The hinged portion of the gallows flooring snapped open with an authoritative thud. A buzz of comment arose from the crowd that was eagerly watching. Satisfied with his test, Sarber called to his deputy who was underneath the gallows flooring:

"Push it up, Jim, it works fine."

Deputy Marshal Jim Messler heaved the hinged flooring into place and checked the iron locking mechanism. The lock had engaged properly.

Marshal Sarber could muster little enthusiasm for the forthcoming hanging. The crime, for which the candidate for the gallows would soon pay, was not particularly heinous by Indian Territory standards. The fact that so many more murderers were footloose and fancy free in the Territory offended the sense of justice the marshal possessed. The forthcoming solitary hanging was poor solace for Sarber's frustration. He pulled a watch from his vest pocket and surveyed the time piece. Replacing it he cast a quizzical eye aloft. Clouds were gathering in the sky, although the scorching rays of the sun were not yet affected. The marshal was awaiting his deputy, who was due in a few seconds to appear with the prisoner—John Childers.

John Childers three years before had slit the throat of an aged peddler, Reyburn Wedding, in the Indian Territory. A resident of the Cherokee Nation and known since childhood as "a bad one," Childers had craved a fine horse that Wedding owned. When the old man refused to part with the animal, Childers calmly knifed him, booted his body into the Caney River, and unhitched the horse from Wedding's ramshackle wagon.

The horse—a showpiece—was well known in the Territory, and it brought about Childers' capture. Deputy Marshal Vennoy, dispatched from the Federal Court located at that time in Van Buren, soon traced Childers to the Creek Nation and captured him. Jailed at Van Buren, Childers soon managed to escape and became a full-fledged outlaw. While he was on the scout, the federal headquarters were moved from Van Buren to Fort Smith. Childers too moved into Fort Smith, leaving his forested lair to slip into town at night and visit a friend in a bawdyhouse.

Deputy Marshal Vennoy was eventually tipped off concerning Childers' nocturnal habits, and he made use of the situation. He made a deal with the prostitute, offering her ten dollars for her help. When Childers arrived for his customary wooing, his ardor was rudely chilled when Vennoy, in company with Deputy Sheriff Joe Peevy, stepped from behind some drapes and handcuffed Childers.

His conviction had been rapid despite a strong fight of the defense. Hosts of witnesses were furnished, claiming to have seen Childers a long distance from the scene of the crime on the day Wedding had died. The murdered Wedding, however, had left a legacy of many friends. Lengthy petitions from those friends had prevented Childers' acquiring clemency. Now he was to hang.

On the sweltering grounds Marshal Sarber again consulted his watch. He raised his eyes, and from his perch on the platform of the big gibbet, he could look over the heads of the hundreds of persons impatiently waiting to see a man hang. Sarber stared toward the court building expectantly.

Exactly on schedule, Deputy Marshal Vennoy appeared at the head of the steps that was the exit from the basement dungeon. He was holding the arm of a stalwart young man whose hands were held forward as though he were praying.

Marshal Sarber, even from the distance across the sea of heads, knew with a certainty that John Childers was not praying. The man's wrists were fettered with heavy iron shackles.

Vennoy, backed by a number of deputies armed with Winchesters, led his man toward the gallows. The packed throng gave way, providing a narrow path.

Soon, Childers was confidently climbing the steps to the platform. The crowd pushed as close around the gallows as it possibly could. Marshal Sarber faced the prisoner and unfolded the death warrant. He read the document slowly and carefully. Raising his eyes, Sarber soberly asked Childers if he had any last remarks.

Childers' bravado was beginning to desert him. It was

becoming apparent that the end for him was definitely in view. From his stance on the gallows platform, Childers talked at great length, remarking that his friends did not seem to be doing anything more to help him. Sarber's lawyer instinct came to the fore:

"Childers, if you will give me the names of your friends, I will promise not to hang you today."

The onlooking mob became tomb-silent as Childers cast an intent gaze around. Everyone knew that somewhere in the immense throng Childers' friends were silent watchers.

Finally, Childers faced Marshal Sarber. The deputy marshals on guard stiffened.

"Didn't you say you were going to hang me?"

Sarber replied in the affirmative.

"Then why in hell don't you!"

Marshal Sarber shrugged. Deputy Marshal Messler unshackled Childers' wrists and bound the man's hands behind his back. The lawman then adjusted the grim, black hood over Childers' head. Sarber raised his arm and gave the signal. Messler jerked the lever and Childers' body shot through the suddenly yawning hole in the platform. He came to a violent stop as he, literally, reached "the end of his rope."

Many in the gaping crowd, however, were not at all convinced. At the same moment a ponderous clap of thunder drowned out all sounds and a vivid streak of lightning flashed from the heavens and struck the massive cross beam of the gallows. A shower of sparks cascaded from the superstructure of the gallows, and the stringent odor of ozone suddenly filled the hot, stifling air.

For a stunned moment no one stirred. John Childers was the only moving thing, quivering at the end of his rope. Then, from dozens of superstitious persons' throats came shrieks of terror. Many turned and blindly raced away to other points. Others melted to their knees and began to pray. Most stood still, with jaws slack in surprise.

Mother Nature again made the next move. With jolting suddenness a hard downpour of rain began. The quick drenching broke the spell, and people ran for cover.

The Childers hanging promptly became a legend, and the gallows took on an aura of superstition that never waned.

The Civil War had stopped the functioning of the Federal Court for the Western District of Arkansas. When military occupation ended at Fort Smith in 1871, the fort was abandoned as a military post and the properties were put under the charge of the marshal. Later that same year, the Federal Court was moved from Van Buren to Fort Smith and the barracks building on the fort grounds was converted into a court headquarters. President Grant appointed Judge Henry J. Caldwell of the Eastern District of Arkansas to take the bench at Fort Smith, and Logan Roots was the marshal. Judge Caldwell efficiently tried the case of John Childers after the felon had been recaptured, and pronounced the hanging decree. While the date for Childers' hanging was pending, William Storey, a lawyer, was appointed to the Fort Smith court as judge in 1872. The powerful carpetbag regime in Arkansas had managed to obtain the appointment for Storey from President Grant. John Sarber became the marshal.

For the Indian Territory, the appointment of Storey proved to be a disaster. Storey was not an adequate man for the job and his administration was riddled with graft and incompetency. Despite the success of the law in capturing, convicting, and hanging John Childers, none of the events could be attributed to Judge Storey, and Marshal Sarber was painfully aware of the fact. Also, he sensed the deep repercussions the bungling court produced on the morale of the deputy marshals who were sworn to venture into the Indian Territory and serve warrants.

With his staff woefully undermanned, and few good lawmen among the men at that, Marshal Sarber was often tempted to tell his befuddled boss to go to hell.

"Seven hundred square miles for the sheriff to police in Johnson County," Sarber would growl, "and I have 74,000 square miles."

Still, the office of marshal—a political plum—was a status of merit, and Sarber was an ambitious man. He stayed on his job.

Sarber had many woes. Witnesses were subpoenaed in large numbers with great abandon, many of them from great distances, and they were supposed to receive certificates of payment for expenses thus incurred. The ludicrous maze of corruption in the court functioning permitted few payments, and most witnesses either had to hock personal belongings or borrow funds in order to return home. Others, sensing financial disaster if they stayed, took off for home while they still had eating money in their pockets. Sarber would be ordered to send deputies after them. The indignant witnesses would be returned to Fort Smith and jailed.

Deputy marshals were not paid a fixed salary. Their income was based on a fee system consisting of reimbursements for expenses and mileage traveled and fees for bringing in wanted criminals and lawbreakers. If a deputy marshal shot a wanted man, he was not only a loser of fees, he had to stand the expense of burying the dead outlaw. With the existing status of payments in the Storey court, the lawmen were understandably hesitant in spending their own money in upholding the law.

With the eyes of a lawyer and a lawman, Sarber saw the irony of the situation at Fort Smith. The Court with awesome jurisdiction was becoming immobile with incompetency at the very time a monstrous crime wave was malignantly enlarging with each passing week in the Indian Territory.

After fourteen months of "Storeyship," Washington stirred. To avoid impeachment, Storey resigned. Of major crimes alone it was ascertained that some fifty murders had occurred in the Indian Territory for which no arrests were made while Judge Storey was on the bench.

Judge Caldwell was transferred from the Eastern District of Arkansas to Fort Smith in a temporary capacity until a permanent judge could be appointed. John Sarber's political post was ended, and he packed his trunk to return to Clarksville and his law practice.

John Childers, number one on the Fort Smith gallows, had departed forever with an insolently flung remark and amid a display of celestial fireworks—a departing as unorthodox as his surroundings. His demise in 1873 heralded a long, long succession of hangings. The resignation of Judge Storey in 1874 opened the way for the beginning of an unprecedented judgeship in the annals of jurisprudence. The law was coming to the Indian Territory, for in 1875, the Iron Judge appeared.

6

THE IRON JUDGE

"This is Fort Smith?"

Having asked her question, Mary O'Toole Parker instinctively reached out a hand for the nearest of her two small sons. The lads were standing with their parents at the rail of a steamboat, and they were engrossed, staring at the strange town on the river bank that had prompted Mrs. Parker's question.

Her husband, whose towering figure was accentuated by the tall beaver hat he wore, noticed the involuntary movement of protectiveness that his wife made as she asked her question.

"Yes, Mary," mused Judge Isaac Charles Parker, "this is Fort Smith."

The judge stepped to the rail in order to get a better view of the dock that the steamboat was approaching. The gap of muddy water narrowed as the boat was brought slowly alongside the heavily constructed platform. High above the judge's head a spurt of steam appeared between the twin stacks of the boat, and a strident hoot of its whistle echoed up and down the wide river. In reverse, the big paddle wheel at the stern thrashed the water vigorously for a moment, killing the remaining forward motion of the steamboat. On the texas deck, the Captain, a megaphone glued to his bearded face, was bellowing orders. Bells in the engine room jangled, lines were heaved and cinched tightly.

The gangplank was shoved out, one end falling to the dock with a crash. The steamboat had arrived at Fort Smith.

From the high deck, Judge Parker could see the top of the sloping river bank that was crowned with a number of shacks. Back from the crest of the slope were the much larger buildings of the town. It was an unseasonally dry period in Arkansas, May 2, 1875, and a pall of dust hung above the town, indicating considerable street traffic. A swarm of people was gathered on the slope to watch the big riverboat land.

Placing two enormous hands on the rail, Parker leaned forward to peer down at the dock. A goodly number of well-dressed citizens stood in a group, separate from the roughly dressed dock hands and lounging frontier characters. A welcoming committee, the judge thought with a wry smile.

Judge Parker was correct concerning the group of town leaders assembled on the dock. They were there to see the new judge, but they were not exactly a welcoming committee, as the judge had facetiously put it. The citizens were merely curious to see the man who was to take William Storey's place on the bench of the United States Court.

Judge Isaac C. Parker was a man born and bred to the frontier way of life. He was born October 15, 1838, in a log cabin in Belmont County, Ohio. Farm life and stern, religious parents provided Parker with a growing-up period of self denial and hard manual labor, but with a bonus. He was encouraged to obtain a basic education. While still in his teens he taught in backwoods schools to earn funds for attending law school. His great amount of "drive" and well-defined purposefulness earned him an admittance to the Ohio Bar in 1859, at the age of twenty-one.

Parker, armed with legal knowledge, yielded to the call of the West. He migrated to St. Joseph, Missouri, and found the place to be an exciting center of frontier activity. The partisan bickerings of the Kansas Jayhawkers and Missouri Bushwhackers often flamed into violence, and young attorney

Parker was an eyewitness to border fury. It was the section of the country in which Jesse James and his gang operated after the close of the war.

Parker began his law practice, and soon married a local girl. He was an able lawyer, and his ambition led him into politics. He served as city attorney and as provost marshal during the war and was a corporal of the home guard. The coming of the war changed Parker's politics. Although he was a Democrat, the hotly debated political issues of the day changed Parker's convictions. As a native of Ohio he was strongly against the institution of slavery, and he became an ardent Republican. Quickly rising as a political power, Parker was first state's attorney and judge of Missouri's Twelfth Judicial Circuit. In 1870, he was elected congressman from the sixth district of Missouri. In Washington, Parker became interested in Indian affairs and was soon regarded as an authority on the knotty subject. With his typically firm convictions, Parker believed in strict fair play by the government in its dealings with the Indian and his problems.

Missouri "went Democratic," and Parker retired from the Washington scene in 1875. Parker had deep convictions concerning men who served the people in governmental capacities and he wanted to serve in an area where a real need existed. Parker's work as a Republican won him an appointment from President Grant. The plum was in the Territory of Utah as chief justice.

Isaac Parker was honored, but he asked for a change in the appointment, to be supplanted with an appointment to the bench of the Federal Court at Fort Smith, Arkansas. Adding weight to Parker's request to the President was the urging of the Arkansas Republican powers; they had spotted an incorruptible and dedicated man in the person of Isaac C. Parker. He was, they figured, just the man needed to repair the damage wrought by a number of detrimental events. The "Brooks-Baxter War" in Arkansas had widened the split in the Republican party, and fiascoes within state government had dealt hard blows to party prestige. Conditions at the Fort Smith Federal Court required immediate corrective action.

On the day of Issac Parker's arrival in Fort Smith, the town fathers gathered at the steamboat dock, expecting the worst. They watched the new judge as he escorted his family down the gangplank. The huge frame of Judge Parker would command the attention of casual observers. The interested watchers noted the genuine courtesy and thoughtfulness the big man extended to his family. They heard the thirty-five-year-old judge's well-modulated baritone voice, and they saw his piercing deep blue eyes and firm jaw. Many openly commented on the judge's broad, powerful shoulders, and nodded approval of the quick, efficient manner that he ordered his luggage placed on the dock. The new judge had a voice that one would expect from a man his size, and the observers could tell that he was accustomed to giving orders and having them obeyed.

But the town fathers allowed Judge Parker to attend to his baggage, and usher his family from the dock, without speaking a word to him. There was no question about the general appearance of Parker, he looked to be a man that no one could push around. However, the "town" chose to "wait and see."

As for Judge Parker, he silently accepted the terms. He moved his family into temporary quarters at the rugged old stone building on the fort grounds that had been built to serve as a powder magazine and commissary. Mary Parker soon discovered that her husband had been correct in his statement of Fort Smith citizens. Some were highly cultured despite the raw appearance of their town. They had lived in the shame of Judge Storey's court long enough to be extremely suspicious of another Republican appointee to the bench. Judge Parker would literally be on trial himself.

His community acceptance or rejection, would follow the verdict of the people.

Judge Parker had been well aware of the conditions at the Fort Smith court when he asked for the job, but he was dumbfounded at the vast number of jailed felons whose cases had not come to trial. The judge soon was even more astonished at the number of felons loose in the Indian Territory who should be prisoners awaiting trials.

Within one week after Parker's arrival, the mill of justice began to creak. Court hours were set for 9 o'clock in the morning until dusk, with one hour off for lunch. It was the beginning of a twenty-one-year grind for Judge Parker.

During the fateful first week eighteen persons came into Judge Parker's court, charged with murder. Fifteen were convicted. Parker sentenced eight of the felons to die on the gallows. Fort Smith, startled, took a new look at the court.

During the lapse of time from the sentencing to the hanging day, September 3, 1875, one of the doomed men made a desperate escape but was immediately brought down by the rifle fire of Deputy Marshal George Maledon. Another gallows candidate was young enough to have pressure brought to bear by persons seeking clemency for him. His sentence was commuted to life imprisonment by presidential decree.

The remaining six were to don the noose:

One, Dan Evans, had desired an excellent horse and fine saddle owned by an eighteen-year-old boy. The boy also dressed in unusually good clothes. When his body, with a bullet in it, was found in the Creek Nation, officers began a search for the expensive chattel. Dan Evans was found, wearing the boy's costly boots.

Another of the six, William Whittington, had ridden to Texas with a friend, and a crock of whiskey. Their supply of spirits running low, the pair returned to the Nations, and Whittington noticed that his friend had $100 when they sought a fresh supply. Far from sober, Whittington knocked his friend from his saddle, cut his throat and stole his money. Officers soon arrested the well-heeled drunk.

Jim Moore was a horse thief and veteran killer. While being pursued by a posse in the Red River country, he shot and killed Deputy Marshal Bill Spivey. The posse soon after captured Moore and brought him back to Fort Smith in irons.

Two of the six were Indians. Smoker Mankiller, a Cherokee, might have been thinking to live up to his name. He called on a neighbor, borrowed his Winchester rifle, and then turned the gun on him. He was quickly apprehended.

Sam Fooey was the other Indian. He observed a young fellow with a well-filled wallet, and went into action. His victim was a schoolteacher who had just been paid $250 for a season of teaching in the Cherokee Nation. Months passed before the skeleton of the teacher was found. The bones were identified by the weathered schoolbooks nearby. Piece by piece, the evidence led the law officers to Fooey.

The sixth prisoner was Edmund Campbell, a Negro. He calmly murdered a farmer and his wife because he thought they insulted him in a conversation.

Amazed at the unfamiliar rate the cases were being handled in the court, Fort Smithians were also delighted to see a man on the bench who spoke with conviction, was impartial, and who obviously sought no political favors. It was a unique and gratifying change, and Judge Parker was accepted. Off the bench Parker was cordial enough, and was rather a soft touch for destitute men with families. Still, Judge Parker was a reserved man when met on the street, as befitted his office. But not with children. Youngsters playing on the streets soon recognized the big judge as a friend.

As the citizens of Fort Smith came to know Judge Parker he was asked to take part in civic affairs. Parker complied where such activities could be handled during evening hours.

He was a member of the Fort Smith Board of Education for years.

Parker surprised Fort Smith again with his first "hanging day." He decreed that the six felons would march to the gallows together! Perhaps this would serve adequate notice to the lawless that a new brand of justice was at hand.

When the day came, a tremendous crowd gathered to view the spectacle. Press notices appeared throughout the nation. On the gallows platform, the six men generally expressed the same sentiments as had John Childers. Some denied their guilt, most were belligerent.

George Maledon proved adept in figuring out the morbid mechanics of a hanging. He made up the nooses and hoods, and in the presence of four clergymen and armed guards on the platform, he jerked the lever. The six murderers shot through the opened floor, and all died instantly with broken necks.

Most residents of the Indian Territory cheered the unusual news from Fort Smith, hoping that a new era of law was indeed at hand. The local presses lauded the event, but most newspapers, especially in the East, made a hullabaloo about the simultaneous hangings. These accounts created "sympathy" for the victims of the nooses, and underplayed the type of country that had bred the killers. Judge Parker was declared, without analyzing the situation facing him, to be cold and unfeeling. It was the beginning of press notices that would frivolously brand him the Hanging Judge.

Parker was little affected by the storm of criticism from distant places. He had already experienced the general misunderstandings of that nature in his dealings with Washington to effect certain changes in his court. He wanted his lawmen placed on an adequate salary, and a suitable jail constructed. Parker was destined to never see the request for lawman salaries materialize, but eventually a new jail was built.

Judge Parker's first efforts at the local level to improve conditions was to insist on recruitment of more deputy marshals. The program brought more lawmen into the service, but there was never to be an adequate number to thoroughly police the huge domain of the court. The number of deputy marshals rose as high as two hundred, but the turnover was rapid. A considerable span of time elapsed before the law enforcers became fully aware that a big change had taken place and that in return for the risks of diligent performance of duty, felons brought to Fort Smith would be placed on trial promptly and efficiently.

Attorneys practicing in Judge Parker's court were aware of the daily chore the big man faced. Many of his problems were present in their profession. Languages, customs, and legal barriers imposed by the Indian Nations were complicated factors to be reckoned with in a court of law. When a prisoner of Indian blood was brought before the bench, he could not, in many instances, understand English. Again, Indians of various tribes would be involved in a case, and none would understand the language of the others. Services of interpreters would be required, and when the jurors became confused on the subject of differing customs in the Territory, it was Parker's job to explain. The Judge was often and vigorously accused of unduly influencing juries. The juries were often composed of rugged frontiersmen who were relatively newcomers in the Indian Territory.

The peace officers of Parker's court soon learned that a forceful man was on the bench and they were aware of his efforts to place them on salaries. Parker took a genuine interest in his men. He made it a point to meet each new deputy marshal unobtrusively and have a chat with him. It was Parker's method of winding up a survey of men who desired to become federal officers in the Territory. The primary attraction to the profession of law enforcement, Parker reasoned, had to be either a love of deadly excitement or a civic desire to aid in improving conditions—or a balanced mixture of both factors. Obviously, fame and fortune were not prime factors, for neither of those plums were existent. Parker sought the "balanced" man.

Consequently, new lawmen who "worked" out of the court presented something of a puzzle to Fort Smith citizens. The cool-eyed deputy marshals were reticent men when it came to gossiping about law work in the Nations. It was observed that frontier-bred men adept with Colt and Winchester did not always get a job, and contrarily, young men with modest backgrounds of pistol and rifle experience were promptly sworn into service at times. The U.S. marshal, however, was quite aware of the hidden hand of Judge Parker in the selection of deputy marshals. The judge wanted dedicated men, but he fully realized the amount of raw courage and accuracy with firearms that the applicant must also possess.

Another unusual factor of the Parker court that set it apart from any other tribunal in the Nation was a peculiarity of judicial circumstances which provided no appeal from Parker's sentences. He was the final arbiter, and a condemned man had no recourse except presidential commutation. The outlaw element as well as the lawmen became cognizant of the Iron Judge. A man wanted for a serious felony in the Indian Nations became a vicious adversary, with an understandable desire to avoid making the "march of the damned" to Fort Smith. Such a journey was tantamount to crawling out on the hinged floor of the big gallows and daring the big judge to pull the lever. The deputy marshals learned that they had the most dangerous type of lawbreaker to contend with—the outlaw who would rather risk a shoot-out than to be taken into custody.

The rugged war between lawmen and outlaws settled down to a deadly hide-and-seek game that would erupt again and again into gun battles. The deputy marshals would load a light wagon with provisions and with spare saddle horses set out from Fort Smith. The Little Rock-Fort

Smith Railroad was completed during the first few years after Parker's appearance in Fort Smith, but it was to be some time before a railroad bridge spanned the Arkansas River. The lawmen would ferry their gear across and enter the Territory with their warrants. Far and wide they would range, at times swearing in possemen when needed. In the remote sections they constantly ran the risk of ambush as their load of prisoners grew. More often than not, darkness would find the lawmen far from a hamlet that offered a hotel and a calaboose for their prisoners. The felons would be chained to the wheels of the wagon, and the deputy marshals would seize a few hours of uneasy sleep. Always, their Winchesters would be across their knees when they were eating, under their hands while they were sleeping and cradled underarm when they were riding.

The lawmen learned that many settlers in the Nations would not offer help. The frontiersman would not see a federal man for months at a time, but an outlaw was apt to drop in most any day. By an unwritten code that favored the outlaw, a settler who evaded questions by deputy marshals was not bothered physically, nor was his livestock stolen. It was a case of survival for the settlers, not a desire to break the law.

Deputy marshals could understand the reticence of farmers and ranchers to provide clues or information. The situation was just a part of the adverse nature of the lawmen's job, but despite the handicaps a steady flow of prisoners was evident at Fort Smith.

Despite the superstitious awe that many people expressed concerning the gallows, the deputy marshals could always depend on a huge crowd come hanging day. The thump of the gallows trap came to be a familiar sound in Fort Smith—to the never-ending consternation of the fainthearted. The huge "engine of destruction," located practically in the residential section of the town, was no doubt a stern object lesson to children. Small boys would break into a run when passing near the grim structure, and none would venture near the premises after dark had fallen. For that matter, many adults had little difficulty in finding business in other locales when dusk came.

Deputy George Maledon became so proficient in preparing the details for a hanging that he, without competitors, was nominated full time to the job. He became known as Parker's Hangman, and he was a perfectionist. He knew just where to place the knot of the noose in order to break a condemned man's neck. "Instant death" was the trade mark of Maledon, he would have considered a "strangulation" a sloppy job. He ordered his ropes from St. Louis, using only the best manila hemp. He would carefully oil and stretch the ropes until there was no give. However, Maledon became a lonely artist, for people avoided him at all times when possible.

No less a perfectionist was Iron Judge Parker. The tremendous vitality of the judge kept the lawyers for the defense and prosecution hopping. The court clerk was forced to live with a case of writer's cramp. Parker did not entertain ideas of eliminating crime entirely; such lofty aims are perhaps reserved for idealists. Parker was a realist, but he was determined to bring majesty to the law again, and in so doing make the Indian Territory a safe, decent place to live.

It was an ambitious goal, one that required a corps of hard-riding lawmen. The law was coming at last to the Indian Territory.

7

THE IRON LAW OF JOHNSON COUNTY

"Bloody Clarksville, indeed!"

James R. Tolbert recalled the words of his wife, and he smiled as he gazed at the sign above his door. It had been three years since he had brought his family to Arkansas. Tolbert placed his hands behind his back, and from his position on the curb edge of the sidewalk in front of his office, he contentedly eyed his sign. It was a huge sign, with letters two feet high, and it was mounted above the door of his newspaper office on Clarksville's main street. Painted in brilliant blue on a white background, the letters of the sign ran the width of the building front, spelling out THE JOHNSON COUNTY HERALD. It was more than just a sign to Tolbert. It was a graphic illustration that he had made a "fair-to-middling" start in his new home town.

Tolbert walked slowly across the sidewalk and entered the door of his office. He kneed open a swinging gate of the counter-high partition dividing the office area and eased himself into his worn old swivel chair.

The words of Tolbert's wife echoed in his memory. Leaving their native Georgia had been a wrench, but it could have been worse. Elizabeth Tolbert had read the lurid news items of Clarksville that had appeared in the Atlanta *Constitution*. It was not so much the move that concerned her—it was the destination.

"It is farther west that the future is best for a man making a new start," Tolbert had argued.

"But to grow up in a town where they shoot people—" she demurred, thinking of the children.

"Clarksville was a prosperous, settled community before the war, and it is on its way back," Tolbert had asserted.

But his wife had not been too far wrong in her opinion of the Arkansas town. In 1880 Clarksville and the surrounding county still felt faint repercussions of the Wallace case. The town was anything but dull, but like buds in the spring, there were definite signs of progress appearing. The coming of the new railroad had livened things up, but the iron fist of a highly efficient sheriff was bringing the unruly elements of society under control.

Tolbert's mood of reveries was suddenly disrupted as a stocky figure bolted through the door of the office.

"I see you still have that circus-sized billboard on your building," roared Bud McConnell.

Tolbert grinned as he kicked a straight cane-bottom chair in the direction of his friend.

McConnell jammed a cheroot in his mouth and took the chair. He applied a match to the cigar, puffing furiously and glaring at Tolbert with twinkling eyes. He had formed a liking for the newspaper man with the Georgia drawl upon first meeting him. "My worthy competitor," as he referred to Tolbert, was an indication of the esteem the fiery sheriff had for the peach-growing editor. The ex-Georgian had good ideas concerning crops, and he was willing to share his knowledge. Tolbert spiced his *Herald* with editorials on the possibilities of agriculture in Johnson County as avidly as McConnell thundered the precepts of law and order in the *Enterprise*.

"How are your Georgia peaches coming along?" Bud inquired.

"Those little trees will be old enough for me to worry about their spring buds before you know it," replied Tolbert, "and there is no reason why that sandy soil on the slopes won't support as many trees per acre—with as big peaches—as any orchard in Georgia."

"Well," observed McConnell, "the slopes around Ludwig will grow peaches, but they are about the size of walnuts."

McConnell was referring to a community four miles northeast of Clarksville where Tolbert had built his home and secured acreage.

"It is the specie of a peach that determines the size," Tolbert explained, "but size means nothing if the flavor is missing. It takes the right kind of soil and climate to produce both."

"I hope your Alberts grow as big as cantaloupes," said Bud.

"Elbertas," corrected Tolbert.

McConnell laughed. "I'm thinking about taking on another profession, too."

Tolbert was surprised. McConnell owned a drugstore and a number of farms in addition to his newspaper and print shop. Along with his office of County Sheriff, McConnell was a busy man.

"I am considering making the race for the state legislature," Bud explained.

Tolbert was interested. "Well, we can use a good man for the county down there in Little Rock. You know where some of your support will be."

McConnell nodded appreciatively. It was good to know that the *Herald* would support him when the time came.

Tolbert greatly admired the forceful sheriff, "the right man for the job who came along at the right time." It was an editorial phrase Tolbert often used, and it was one that he firmly believed in.

McConnell was a man with boundless energy. Two years before the Tolberts arrived in Clarksville, in 1878, he had made the race for sheriff, and won the contest easily. Since the climax of the Wallace case he had promoted the cause

of a firm law enforcement program with editorials. Whenever
the need or opportunity presented itself he volunteered for
posse duty.

"In the saddle" after his successful race for the sheriff's
office, Bud promoted a designed concept of law enforcement. He carefully selected his deputies, studying each
aspirant for the job and interrogating him fully. McConnell's deputies followed a general pattern of personality, they
were "quiet" men, not given to much talk. Bud set the pace
for them.

First to feel the effects of the "new system" were the
saloons. A sharp decrease in expenditures for new window
glass occurred almost overnight. At the sound of the first
pistol shot of the evening, or even loud, rude talking, McConnell would enter the offending saloon and collar the troublemaker without preliminaries. He would promptly "rooster-
walk" the offender to a jail cell, and only the payment of
a fine for disturbing the peace could effect a release. For
McConnell, it was a valuable example that he set for his
deputies. It was a last test to assure the sheriff that he had
made a wise choice of personnel selection. Bud wanted men
who could do their part in cleaning up and policing the
community and county without becoming "obligated" to
any citizen, rich or poor. A minor peace disturbance case
provided a good testing field, Bud reasoned.

The concentration of deputies on the antics of the chronic
peace disturbers brought immediate improvement of Clarksville's evening conduct. From the time the street lamps were
lit until the dawn grayed the night sky, the silent deputies
were on the job. The saloon boys soon learned that it was a
lot cheaper, as the evening's gaiety soared to a climax, to
simply ease out the door and stagger sedately home or to
the friendly darkness of the livery barn.

With would-be outlaws, the stocky sheriff was utterly
merciless. The tough element in the county as well as the
town was not long in learning to respect Bud McConnell

and his hard-eyed deputies. If a man was suspected of having a connection with a shooting or lawbreaking affair, Bud figured that the thing to do was to get him into town for sizing up. With a deputy or two, Bud would ride out to a suspect's home, or lair, and bluntly order him to "grab his hat and saddle up." The new precedent of law enforcement encouraged outraged people to file the proper complaints, instead of taking the law into their own hands. Just as Bud figured it would, the entire legal structure of the county took heart.

To help in this new campaign, McConnell sought out a tall, broad-shouldered young man who was making quite a name for himself as city marshal of the town of Coal Hill, in the western part of the county fourteen miles from Clarksville. Coal Hill had a saloon in practically every other building in the business district. Coal mines in the area were in full swing, and many rough miners sought noisy recreation in the town. It was a wild and rowdy town, a fertile field to breed shooting affrays until the new city marshal went into action. The city lawman had been pressed into taking the job by worried responsible citizens in Coal Hill. A newcomer from Madison County, his first visit to the town was marred when a group of miners attempted to "rawhide" him. The stalwart stranger was the wrong man for a bunch of drunks to pick on. They were laid low by a flailing new ax handle that the stranger purchased for the occasion.

The city marshal had accepted the job, for he was appalled at the dangerous situation where even a peaceful fellow could not step into a saloon for a quick drink without being messed up. To bring about peaceful conditions, he simply clubbed the tough miners into submission and dragged them off to confinement. Plenty of muscle and raw courage were required for a lone man to get away with such deeds; it was a language the miners understood, and peace came suddenly to the noisy little mining center.

"Got to have that man," McConnell vowed, and in 1880

he appointed James F. "Bud" Ledbetter a Johnson County deputy sheriff.

McConnell quickly realized that Ledbetter was a "born" lawman. The two "Buds" often ranged the length and breadth of the county together in search of dangerous quarry. Folks in the caned river bottoms to the south, in the rolling, thickly forested Ozark Mountains to the north, the Piney Creek area to the east, and among the burgeoning coal mines westward—all were aware that a hard-riding bunch of lawmen was on duty in the county. Hard-cases knew that "those laws in Clarksville weren't fooling around."

J. R. Tolbert had more than an editor's interest in law enforcement. His oldest son, Paden, was vitally interested in the activities of Bud McConnell and Bud Ledbetter. Stories of the days of Sid Wallace intrigued Paden, and he was an authority on the subject.

"Perhaps," mused Tolbert, "it was the way we raised the boy that makes him so interested in the causes of rough and dangerous times."

Young Paden had received the best education possible in Georgia, despite Tolbert's limited means. The stubborn father even swore off the use of cheroots for long periods of time in order to provide his older sons with "school britches" and shoes.

Paden Tolbert's schooling had provided him with a job. School Commissioner Littlebury Robinson offered him a post teaching school, and Paden took it. However, his father easily detected a restless spirit in the young man. In line with the vogue of the era, Paden had carefully nurtured an adolescent mustache that now was thick and stylish. The mustache though, was just about the only nod to the customs of most young men of the day that Paden Tolbert permitted himself to make. Aside from perfunctory attendance to play-parties, even those sponsored by the school, the young teacher preferred a life out of doors. At every opportunity he volunteered for posse duty and became fa-

miliar with the remote corners of the county. From his
meager salary he purchased a fine Colt .45 single action
Army Model six-shooter. The weapon sported a pair of
ivory grips with carved steer heads in bas-relief.

J. R. Tolbert sighed the dismay countless fathers before
him had expressed when they suspected that the first-born
was not following the paternal footsteps. Tolbert's peach
trees were growing sturdily, but he knew that it would be
some time in the too distant future before the orchard would
begin bearing fruit and call for his full time.

Bud McConnell's dream of changing professions was having trouble materializing too. On March 7, 1883, the Little
Rock-Fort Smith Railroad suffered a holdup, or more ac-
curately, the train was shot up.

When the westbound train stopped for passengers at Mulberry, a town some thirty miles west of Clarksville, four
characters ambled nonchalantly aboard. They were Jim
Johnson, Monroe MacDonald, Gove Johnson, and James
Herndon. They found seats in a coach, and as they were
average-appearing young men, the other passengers gave
them little heed. As the train began to move, the four men
pulled large bandannas from their pockets. They adjusted
the big kerchiefs to form masks for their faces.

Conductor Cain came down the aisle of the coach,
methodically punching tickets. He paused in astonishment
before the masked group.

"We ain't got no money or tickets," leered one of the men.

Conductor Cain promptly raised his hand to grasp the
emergency cord near the ceiling of the coach. Before he
could jerk the cord, one of the bandits snaked a Colt out of
his waistband and thumbed a quick shot. The conductor,
with his arm stretched over his head, was hit squarely. He
fell backward, killed instantly.

The crash of the large-caliber revolver was a thunderclap
in the confines of the coach. Through the haze of smoke
from the shot the bandits could see the white faces of the

passengers staring with horrified eyes at the inert form of the trainman.

Brakeman Lester heard the boom of the shot from another coach, and he decided to investigate. When he entered the smoky coach containing the masked men, one of the outlaws fired another shot. The bullet creased the trainman's head nastily, and the impact sent him spinning to the floor. Several women passengers recovered their voices and began to scream wildly, and if the outlaws had a plan, it suddenly went awry. They bolted, scrambling for the vestibule, and tangled with each other in the narrow aisle. In their excited struggles with themselves the bandits began firing their guns. Bullets whacked into the woodwork of the coach, and a few leaden slugs crashed the glass of a couple of windows. One wild bullet thumped into the tin stovepipe of the cast-iron monkey stove in the forward part of the coach. The frail pipe fell apart, spraying the adjacent passengers with soot. The air was now fogged with dense gun smoke, and male passengers, with hoarse shouts, made dives for the floor. Above the din the piercing shrieks of women could be heard.

Reaching the vestibule of the coach, the outlaws, with wild abandon, flung themselves from the now rapidly moving train.

The frightened passengers began sawing on the emergency cord, and the train was brought to a jolting stop. Except for scratches caused from flying wood splinters and fragments of glass, none of the excited passengers were injured. The wounded brakeman was bleeding badly, and after a hasty consultation, the trainmen decided to back the train to Mulberry in order to secure medical attention as quickly as possible. The engineer opened his throttle as far as it would go, so that the train would be moving too fast for boarding when it passed the spot where the outlaws had made their exit.

Half expecting to undergo a fusillade of shots as the train chugged rapidly past the place where the bandits had jumped, the passengers peered fearfully at the dense thickets near the track. However, the outlaws evidently were through with the train, and there was no sign of them to be seen.

The train quickly made its reverse run to Mulberry, and the authorities were notified. A number of passengers were certain that one of the bandits had accidentally wounded a companion during the excited gun play. A hastily formed posse was dispatched at once to the site on the tracks, and the injured man was soon located, hiding under a bush. He had been deserted by his friends, for he was in no condition to ride. The bandits had hidden horses near the place so they could flee after the holdup.

Although the shooting had occurred in Franklin County, Bud McConnell sent two of his crack deputies to the neighboring county to lend a hand. Bud Ledbetter and John Powers with a carefully chosen young posseman loaded their horses aboard the next westbound train and journeyed to the site of the holdup.

Ledbetter and Powers, already experienced manhunters, went to work. The fact that the outlaws had bothered to mask themselves after boarding the train stamped them as amateurs, but with a murder charge now hanging over their heads, they would be extremely dangerous men to corner.

The captured bandit flatly refused to divulge any information, despite having been left behind by his companions, but it did not take Ledbetter long to locate the site where the horses of the outlaws had been staked out. Trampled ground and horse droppings were easily found, but a trained eye was required to spot the trail leading away from the site. Finding the trail, the three lawmen knew that the wanted men had fled northward to the densely forested mountains.

Powers wired Bud McConnell that an extensive pursuit appeared to be in the offing. The lawmen rented a mule and loaded it with supplies. A sack of corn meal was added for the horses and mule, for green-up time had just come to the mountain and livestock forage would still be sparse. Several boxes of ammunition were added to the mule's burden.

The *Johnson County Herald* followed the adventures of the lawmen as closely as was possible for J. R. Tolbert's son Paden was the young posseman with Powers and Ledbetter.

Clarksville citizens read the *Herald* accounts of the manhunt with zest for three weeks. The lawmen followed the trail of the bandits on a zig zag course back and forth across the ridges of the Ozark Mountains. The trail often crossed itself, until finally, the pursuers sighted their quarry. The ragged and unkempt outlaws gave up in disgust.

"Hell," grumbled one weary gunman, "those bastards would of chased us to Kingdom Come."

Jailed at Ozark, Arkansas, the county seat of Franklin County, the public defender was successful in requesting a change of venue. The trial was held in Johnson County, which was a mistake for the welfare of the outlaws, for they were sentenced to hang for the murder of Conductor Cain.

The wounded gunman, now fully recovered, would make a total of four who would march to the gallows. The little indoors gallows of the Johnson County courthouse in Clarksville was deemed to be too slow for the task at hand. Bud McConnell ordered a special gallows erected near the railroad depot in the southeast part of the town. The temporary gibbet was designed to accommodate its candidates quickly and efficiently.

The date for the hanging of the Franklin County outlaws was set June 22, 1883, but a few days prior to the big event, a state-wide convention of county sheriffs was scheduled in Little Rock. During the convention, Bud McConnell was one of the speakers. While addressing the assembly he mentioned that he would shortly hang four condemned men. Noting the round of applause that greeted his remarks, he extended an invitation to the entire body of lawmen to come to Clarksville and witness how Johnson County "enforced the law." Forty-two sheriffs accepted his offer.

T. Hartman, the former conductor on the Little Rock-Fort Smith train, had been promoted to the post of superintendent. Sheriff McConnell's sweeping invitation to convention attendants received quite a play in the Little Rock newspapers, and Hartman sent a message to McConnell's hotel; the railroad company could provide a special coach for such an interesting trip. Bud accepted the offer.

The special coach was attached to the train bound for Clarksville; soon the small army of sheriffs was assembled at the spanking new gibbet. Bud McConnell took charge of the situation. He ordered the undertaker's wagon to be pulled away at a discreet distance from the gallows. He then requested the town's three physicians to mount the steps to the platform and called for a minister. One of Bud's deputies informed him that a preacher was over in the jail with the condemned men. Bud tilted his black Stetson to the back of his head and fired up a cheroot. He leaned against the pillar of the gallows to wait for his deputies to arrive with the four prisoners.

A member of the train crew walked up and handed Sheriff McConnell a large envelope. As the man walked away, Bud straightened up and tore the envelope open. It was a statement, signed by Superintendent Hartman, for the use of the special coach. The amount of the bill was $125—the exact amount the railroad company had asked for the use of its train nine years ago, when Bud had commandeered it.

For a moment Bud's big mustache quivered as his heavy jaw clamped the cheroot in his mouth. Then he removed the cheroot and let out a great, booming laugh.

The visiting sheriffs were startled, they could see nothing comical in a situation where four men were about to die, and the townspeople in the big crowd were puzzled. They knew that their sheriff was not given to humor when performing certain official tasks.

However, by the time the prisoners were arranged on the platform of the gallows, the sheriff was his usual self. He pulled the trap level of the gallows in a calm and methodical manner.

Enforcing the law often proved to be grim business for Bud McConnell. One day a huge Negro ran amuck and raped the wife of one of the town's leading citizens. Bud was successful in quickly apprehending the fellow, but he misjudged the volatile and unpredictable nature of a mob that quickly formed. Clarksville's mob was as mindless as any large crowd bent on a vague idea of revenge. As usual, a few loud-voiced men, crazed with excitement, set the pace, and the jail was stormed. Bud McConnell was trussed up like a mummy, and the cell door was opened. The prisoner was carried bodily to the rear of the jail and hung from the limb of a small tree.

On another occasion, a miner in the coal mining community of Spadra, near Clarksville, was involved in an altercation. Reporting to the scene, Sheriff McConnell noticed the miner was holding a loaded and cocked shotgun. McConnell asked the fellow to hand over the weapon.

"You'll have to come and get it," grated the miner.

"All right," McConnell answered calmly, "but you had better hand it over."

When the sheriff started toward the miner, he leveled the shotgun, and Bud dropped him instantly with a precisely aimed shot.

Despite the grimness of law enforcement, McConnell managed to keep his excellent sense of humor. J. R. Tolbert was one of the few citizens of Clarksville who grasped the fact that the brusque, efficient Johnson County sheriff harbored a deep love of wit and humor. As editors, they often exchanged ideas of community problems and possible solutions. On subjects of law enforcement, Tolbert often mentioned his son's affinity for posse work.

"Paden will work in the orchard," mused Tolbert, "but I

have an idea that he simply likes to be out in the open, rather than expressing any regard for a young peach tree."

Bud McConnell laughed. "You did a fine job raising that boy. He's a perfect gentleman, serious about anything he undertakes to do. But there is as much Old Nick in him as there is in you and me. Reckon that is why I thought he would make a good posseman. It takes a well-rounded man to make a first-class lawman."

Tolbert nodded, pleased with the compliment. He remembered Bud McConnell's lecture when Paden, bored with being a teacher, broached him for a job as a posseman.

"Son," McConnell had barked, "I am more interested in why a man wants to be a lawman than in hearing how good he thinks he will be on the job. What's your reason?"

Paden's level, blue-eyed stare had matched Bud's fierce gaze.

"A lawman is a necessary part of a community, especially in a community that can go bad unless there is a good man with a badge to stop it."

McConnell was satisfied. He took a liking for the muscular young man with the thick Georgia drawl.

"We'll see how you work out. There is no place for a bully with a badge in Johnson County. But, if you don't get results from a reasonable request, use your best judgment. I will insist on crack shooting if you have to shoot. See that you get plenty of practice."

McConnell received considerable ribbing from loafers on the courthouse square concerning his choice of a "polite schoolteacher" for posse work. Bud, however, had made it a point to personally observe his new "student" on the job.

"Cool as a cucumber," was Bud's verdict.

Following McConnell's advice, Paden bought as much ammunition for his new six-shooter as his meager schoolteaching salary permitted. He practiced with determination and soon Bud Ledbetter took an interest. Paden became his boon companion and apt pupil. By the time Bud McConnell got his long desired chance to enter other fields of endeavor, in 1885, Paden was a master with Winchester and Colt.

Bud McConnell's successor was W. S. Jett, a prominent young man in the town. He shared the views of McConnell that a solution to lawlessness lay in the effectiveness of a law enforcement body. When Jett announced he would be a candidate for the sheriff's office, McConnell welcomed the opportunity. At last, he had a man he could endorse, and with that endorsement Jett won the race.

Jett never created a doubt of his ability, he was a "McConnell man," and he exhibited the same iron drive of his predecessor. October 7, 1885, shortly after he took the office of sheriff, he appointed Paden Tolbert to be one of his deputies.

At the beginning of that year J. R. Tolbert became a "full-time" orchardist. However, a newspaper man never loses his nose for news. The elder Tolbert kept abreast of Fort Smith news. Perhaps he had a father's premonition that sooner or later, Paden would look to the law enforcement possibilities that the Indian Territory offered.

The big news in Fort Smith in the year of 1886 was Judge Parker's new gallows. Thirty-four felons had stretched rope on the old gallows, and a new gibbet was believed to be in order, for the now world-famous court was functioning steadily, with no signs of letting up. Men had been hung by twos and threes, and more than once the full capacity of six had been utilized.

Martin Luther Stoufer, a master woodworker and owner of the Mechanics Planing Mill in Fort Smith, had built many of the fine staircases and interior wood finishes of the town's leading homes and large buildings. He contracted to build a new gallows.

The new gibbet was an even larger monster than the preceding one. Constructed on the same design, it had a capacity of sending twelve men simultaneously to eternity. Stoufer was a skilled workman and a practical man, but even he was aware of the dread atmosphere of death at the gallows site. Built on the same foundations as the old one, the new structure had only twelve steps leading to the platform instead of the conventional thirteen.

There was little superstition in the make-up of J. R. Tolbert. He was now more concerned with weather conditions and watching for orchard blights than with news material, but the news of the new gallows at Fort Smith affected him. The new gibbet simply meant that there was more to come.

The former editor's premonition was well founded. By the time lawlessness approached its peak in the Indian Territory, his son would be on the scene.

8

THE MARSHALS RIDE

Deputy Marshal Dan Maples was riding to his death. The
chain of events began when he received a letter at his home
in Bentonville, Arkansas. The letter was from Marshal John
Carroll at Fort Smith, requesting immediate investigation of
wholesale whiskey selling in and around Tahlequah, in the
Indian Nations.

Although it was less than twenty-five miles from Bentonville due west to the Indian Territory border, Tahlequah was
fifty miles away in a southwesterly direction. No railroad
had yet been built that offered convenience to Maples' proposed route. He hitched a team to his camp wagon and
started out.

Dan Maples urged his team along at a steady gait for
the remainder of the day. At least the capital town of the
Cherokee Nation boasted a telephone and a line to Fort
Smith. He would be able to keep in touch with the marshal.
Maples was familiar with the road and trails that he was
following, and he decided to let the team walk for a couple
of hours in the bright night before he set up his camp.

During the middle of the following day, May 5, 1887, he
arrived in Tahlequah. Maples arranged with a livery stable
for the care of his team, and then he sought out a modest
hotel. He washed away the travel dust, and took stock
of the changeable spring weather. The day had turned off
hot and humid, and Maples exchanged his heavy clothing for

a pair of brown striped trousers and a white shirt that set off his dark good looks.

Tahlequah was the focal point of the Cherokee Nation, and perhaps the most colorful city of the Five Civilized Tribes. Tahlequah had a newspaper that was published in English and Cherokee, and the dissemination of news to the tribal members was far advanced over the other Nations. As with other tribes, the Cherokee Constitution prevented double jeopardy, imprisonment for debts, conviction without trial by jury, and confiscation of property.

Maples was well informed on Indian tribal law, which had no jurisdiction over crimes involving only white men within the Territory. As a deputy marshal, he was not concerned with crimes committed by Indians against Indians; the Indian police—Lighthorsemen—were quite adept in the enforcement of their laws.

With its imposing Cherokee Council House situated in the center of the town, Tahlequah was indeed a colorful little city.

Refreshed from the rigors of his trip, Maples went to work and soon had a list compiled of the more persistent offenders of the federal whiskey law. As the day was waning he went to the store of James Stapler, merchantman and postmaster, who also had charge of the town's telephone. Maples informed Stapler that he wanted to place a call to the marshal's office in Fort Smith, but that he wanted to do the calling after the store, a busy location in the town, had closed for the day. Informed that an hour would pass before the store would be empty of customers, Maples decided to take a look at Big Springs, a location on the north edge of town that derived its name from a spring that was the headwaters of Spring Branch.

Nancy Shell owned a cabin at Big Springs, and she apparently had many visitors. Maples wanted to check out the place to see if he could find a clue to the source of her liquid stock.

Dusk was falling as the deputy marshal sighted the lighted windows of the cabin. Just in front of him was a footbridge that spanned Spring Branch. It was warm and humid among the big trees that towered in the gloom above the path, and Maples paused to turn up the cuffs of his white shirt and loosen his string tie. At that moment, the door of the cabin opened, spilling a yellow glow from the lighted interior.

Two figures stepped out of the open door; one was exceptionally tall, and the other was of medium size. In the momentary flash of light that shone on the two men, Maples recognized the shorter person. He was John Parris, one of the names on the list. In the gloom of the late evening the two men became shadow figures as the cabin door closed behind them. They advanced in the direction of Maples, evidently aiming to take the path across the footbridge and thence to town.

As the two men approached they were talking loudly, and the taller figure stumbled clumsily on the smooth path, eliciting much mirth from the pair.

The men were still a good fifty feet away when Maples, stepping out on the footbridge, called out for them to stop.

The two figures jerked to a halt with startled gasps. Then they wheeled and began running toward the cabin. Maples quickly slipped his six gun from its holster and fired a warning shot in the air. The fleeing men stopped and crouched in the waist-high grass bordering the path. In the dim light they could see the white gleam of Maples' shirt. In an instant a flash of orange fire jutted from the huddled figures, and the bellow of a large-caliber revolver jarred the air. Dan Maples toppled from the one-plank bridge and fell with a splash face down in the shallow stream. He did not move.

With whispered words in Cherokee, the two men raced to the stream. One stooped and rolled the limp body over. There was just enough light remaining for them to see the heavy silver badge pinned to the sodden shirt front. Silence was heavy in the humid air after the racket of the gunshot. The two figures, one erect and the other crouched over the body in the water, were not aware that the light in the nearby cabin was suddenly extinguished.

Casting aside the shock of seeing the law badge, the two men leaped into the brush downstream from the bridge, and the crash of their frantic progress died away into the distance.

Gradually, the night insects began their faint sounds again, and somewhere upstream, a little frog croaked a query. The body in the water, obstructing the flow of the narrow stream, was motionless. Maples' death was not discovered until daylight, and then Tahlequah was alive with speculation. A number of hard-cases, nervous from recent brushes with the law, saddled up and fled. They wanted no part of a charge of killing a deputy marshal.

Dan Maples had been an exceptionally well-liked man in Bentonville, and that town offered a $500 reward for the capture of the killer. The governor of Arkansas also promoted a reward.

Investigations at Tahlequah quickly led to Nancy Shell's cabin door. The persistence of the officers finally forced the information from Nancy that a fellow by the name of Parris was one of the two men who visited her cabin "just before two shots were heard." However, Nancy would not or could not identify the other man.

The first deputy marshal to push an investigation of the murder of Dan Maples was Heck Thomas. He arrested Charlie Bobtail, a Cherokee lawbreaker who had just completed a penitentiary sentence. Although Thomas knew that Bobtail had nothing to do with the Maples case, he had information that Parris was a close friend of Bobtail's. Bobtail had had his fill of law enforcement, and he was not anxious to become involved in anything that might cause his return to prison. He told Heck Thomas where Parris could be found, and the officers soon had the wanted man in custody.

Bobtail and Parris were formally arraigned on a charge of murder, and, as Thomas had guessed, Parris turned state's evidence. He completely cleared Bobtail of any complicity in the Maples murder and named Ned Christie as his companion on the night of the shooting in front of Nancy Shell's cabin. Christie, Parris swore, was the one who jerked out a revolver and killed Maples.

Ned Christie proved at the outset to be an enigmatic man. He was the son of Watt Christie, and a full-blooded Cherokee. His formal education had been rather skimpy, and he spoke English brokenly, as did most Cherokee men his age, but he understood the language perfectly. He was a gunsmith by profession, as was his father, and he had the reputation of being an outstanding marksman with firearms in an era when good shots were the rule. He was well liked by his fellow tribesmen and was elected to a post of Advisor on the Cherokee Council. He also served as a bodyguard for the Principal Chief, Dennis Bushyhead.

Christie's judgment was considered sound, and those who sought his services both as a tradesman and government figure were well satisfied with his work. At thirty-four years of age, Christie was a striking figure of manhood, dark features, snapping black eyes and he wore his hair in long black locks contrary to most Cherokees. He was six feet four inches in height, and he had the catlike agility of his forebears.

It was general knowledge however, that Christie could be dangerous when aroused. A couple of years before the Maples murder, he had become involved in a quarrel with an Indian named Palone. A fight developed during which Christie knifed and killed his opponent. He was tried by the Cherokee government and acquitted.

It was well known that Ned Christie liked his whiskey and was always on the lookout for choice frontier red-eye.

Ned Christie was in a quandary. For two days he had remained at his home, twelve miles east of Tahlequah, since the nightmare evening when he had fired at the ghostly white object in the dusk. The dull silver of the deputy marshal's badge on the soiled white shirt was burned into his memory. Christie had told his wife of the shooting of Dan Maples. Although her impassive Cherokee features hid her forebodings, Christie knew she was aware of the gravity of the situation.

Ned had little to do about his place. His sixteen-year-old son Arch managed the few chores, caring for a cow, chickens, and three horses. Ned gazed from his window at his small garden that was neatly laid out and becoming lush in the warm spring sunshine. His wife and son would have little tending now, and the products would soon be edible.

In deep thought, Ned turned from the window and opened a cupboard. He removed a pair of large revolvers and placed them on the kitchen table. He got out his cleaning kit and carefully began to clean and oil the weapons. Ned's father had carried the arms while soldiering during the Civil War. Though the blue finish was worn, the six-shooters were in excellent condition. They were .44-caliber Colts.

Ned rubbed the sleek surface of the guns with an oily cloth. When he had asked his father for the revolvers, he had been studying the method the Colt factory used in rebuilding the 1861 Model Army revolver to handle the popular .44-caliber cartridge. Christie carefully copied the method, making his own conversion from percussion ignition to breech loader. Painstakingly, he milled away the metal of the cylinders by means of his foot-operated gunsmith's lathe, removing the rearward portion of each cylinder that contained the percussion cap nipples. He reworked the hammers of the pieces, installing firing pins, and he ordered a pair of new barrels from the Colt factory. The barrels contained spring-loaded ejection rods for removing spent shells. With Ned's remodel job, the six guns were on a par with

Colt's later model single action revolver that used metallic ammunition.

Completing his cleaning operations, Ned fed five big brass cartridges into the cylinder of each gun. His mind was made up. Calling to his son to saddle a horse, Ned buckled on his gun belt and holster. He slipped one revolver into the worn holster and shoved the other into his waistband.

Christie put his mount into a hungry lope that rapidly ate up the distance to Tahlequah. He went straight to the rooming house where he maintained quarters during the week to facilitate his councilor work. A fellow councilman also had a room in the house, and Ned went to his friend's quarters. Ned learned that Deputy Marshal Thomas had succeeded in making Parris talk. Christie had been named as the killer of Deputy Marshal Dan Maples.

Ned's friend soberly advised that under no circumstances should he permit himself to be taken to Fort Smith.

Ned stared at his friend. The man's reasoning made sense. The shooting of a white man, and a federal officer at that, would place Christie beyond the pale of the Cherokee law— he would have to answer to Judge Parker.

But Christie was angered at the mere thought of being a wanted man. As soon as darkness fell, he rode out of town and headed for his home. He was evidently not detected during his visit to town for there were no pursuers on his trail.

Deputy marshals were not long in determining that Christie must be in or near his home. A number of lawmen individually attempted to approach Ned's house, but Christie was always warned well in advance. There were large numbers of Cherokees who believed that Ned was innocent of premeditated murder, and they thoroughly appreciated his reluctance to face Judge Parker. The trap door of the big gallows at Fort Smith was thudding with deadly regularity. The Cherokees rallied with silent vigor to protect Ned.

Ned quickly established himself with the federal law as

being a dangerous quarry. With his self-appointed sentries,
the lawmen found a difficult situation existed. If an officer
did get within shouting distance of Ned's house, the only
answer to a call for surrender was a zipping bullet coming
too close for comfort. It was suicidal for a man to expose
himself to view. There was no question about it. Christie
was something of a hero to the inhabitants. The retreating
lawmen had the uncomfortable feeling that they were permitted to retire safely from the scene only by the grace of
Christie's hidden friends.

It was an embarrassing stalemate for the deputy marshals.
The rolling hills of the Going Snake District were heavily
forested, giving Christie and his friends every advantage
against surprise attacks. Christie could not have picked a
better section of the Cherokee Nation to make his stand.
Figuring that Christie had received ample warning, the
lawmen ceased attempting to take him alive.

Christie was well aware of the change of tactics. He
went to the home of Eli Wilson, a close friend who lived a
mile and a half north of the Christie homestead. Wilson,
Christie knew, had just purchased a new Winchester Model
73, in .44-40 caliber. Christie wanted to buy that weapon.
His old rifle was in .58-55 caliber and would provide his
house with an excellent defender. The new rifle used cartridges that were interchangeable with the ammunition required for his six-shooters, and it would make an ideal rifle
to carry in a saddle boot.

Christie succeeded in purchasing the coveted rifle, and
with the help of his son, he prepared his home for defense.
He set up extra containers to hold water, eliminating trips
to the spring in case of a siege. He fashioned four large
leather pouches. Designed to hold cartridges, the pouches
had rawhide loops so they could be carried, suspended by
the loops around the wearer's neck, much like the nail pouch
of a carpenter's apron. Hand-loaded ammunition in boxes
was also placed at strategic points about the house. Powder

and buckshot were provided for the muzzle-loading Springfield musket that Ned utilized for a shotgun.

When Ned's vigilant neighbors sped a dispatcher to him
with an alarm, Ned would don two ammunition pouches
and his son would put on the other two. Christie's wife
would check the water containers, filling those that were
low. If Christie sighted an intruder, he would draw a careful
bead and send a slug whizzing viciously within inches of a
lawman's head, disdaining to attempt a kill with the first
shot. If he had to fire again, Christie was shooting for scores.

Eli Wilson's small son and other children in the area
would hear sounds of gunfire. When the firing ended the
children would go over to the Christie place and pick up
shiny brass empty shells. Ned was happy to retrieve the expensive items; he could reload them. If the lawmen had
returned fire, the children would search the forest in attempts to find ejected shells for Ned. On these occasions,
Ned greatly enjoyed playing a game of marbles with the
assembled children.

Ned Christie was a great believer in the Indian fortune-
teller's predictions, and often he would gird for battle upon
being warned from that source. Otherwise, Ned depended
solely on the elaborate grapevine system that had developed
in the area.

With Ned secluded in his impenetrable fastness, time
went by. Within two years the rewards on his head came
to $1500. Deputy Marshal Heck Thomas, on a visit to the
Cherokee Nation, decided to have a try at capturing Christie.

For his part, Ned Christie was more than determined to
resist any efforts to take him to Fort Smith. Judge Parker
had at last been successful in obtaining a new jail. A three-
story bastille was constructed adjoining the former barracks
building that housed the court. The old dungeon cells fell
into disuse, and the court was now girded to face the last
decade of the nineteenth century. It was the year of 1889,

and the judge now was following the Christie case closely. He was aware of the attempt that Heck Thomas was planning.

Heck Thomas enlisted the aid of L. P. "Bones" Isbel, a seasoned deputy marshal of Vinita, I.T., who knew the Cherokee country well. The two marshals secured three possemen, and Heck laid out a master plan. The lawmen would enter the "Christie country" from divergent points, hoping to elude detection by Christie "sentries," and meet at a spot near Christie's home.

The project was carried out in the darkness of a late night. The lawmen converged at the planned location, and they were certain that they had not been detected. It was an hour before daybreak when they crept up to Christie's house, but their hopes for a surprise were suddenly dashed. Christie's dogs set up a furious barrage of barking.

The awakened Christie raced to the loft of his house and kicked a board loose from a gable end to provide a vantage point for observation and firing. The lawmen hastily sought the nearest available cover.

Christie began taking pot shots at every dim movement he could observe. His bullets were zipping near live targets.

Heck Thomas had no desire to be pinned down until daybreak and then be forced to retreat. In a few minutes an idea came to him. Christie's gunshop was contained in a small structure near the house. Heck had heard that it was well equipped with a lathe, forge, and other necessary tools for gunsmithing.

Surely, Heck thought, Christie will not stand by and see his shop burn.

Heck cupped his hands to his mouth and shouted to Christie:

"Surrender, or send your wife out. If we fight, I am going to set your gunshop afire."

Christie's reply was a blast from his Winchester.

Heck Thomas was not a man easily daunted. He had already won a name on Parker's force aside from his reputation before coming to the Indian Territory. His life had been filled with violence since his twelfth birthday when he became a courier in his uncle's Brigade of the Army of General Robert E. Lee. As a railroad agent in Texas in the immediate years following the war, he had so doggedly trailed outlaw Sam Bass that the railroad company had presented him with a gold watch. His Texas exploits had easily won him a berth on Parker's force. On one occasion Thomas astonished even Judge Parker by bringing in to Fort Smith a wagon containing thirty manacled prisoners.

Heck Thomas wasted no more words with Ned Christie. He crawled up to a wall of the gunshop and piled material for kindling. Setting the stuff afire, he retreated to the safety of the woods. Deputy Marshal Isbel was covering his actions, firing from first one side of a tree, and then the other. In making the shift, Isbel accidentally exposed one shoulder. Instantly, the eagle-eyed Christie sent a rifle ball smashing through the shoulder. Knocked off balance by the impact, Isbel stumbled backward and sat down. Heck turned his attention to his wounded comrade, and at that instant, Christie's wife, racing with the speed of a frightened fawn, left the house and vanished into the woods.

The flames from the burning shop caught Heck's eye as he was tearing a piece of cloth to make a bandage. A dawn breeze had kicked up suddenly, bending tendrils of fire against Christie's house. In a few minutes, the house was ablaze.

A figure erupted suddenly from the door of the blazing house and sprinted for the woods. Thinking it was Christie, Heck snatched up his Winchester and shouted a command to halt. The fleeing figure did not hesitate, and just before it disappeared into the woods, Heck fired.

Heck knelt again to take care of Isbel's wound. The marshal was bleeding badly, and fast becoming groggy from loss of blood. Thomas applied his crude bandage, and with the help of the three possemen, placed Isbel on his horse.

At this moment, Heck noticed a movement at the front part of the burning house. It was Christie. The Cherokee broke into a loping run for the timber. The flickering glow from the burning house provided a bright but deceptive light. Grabbing up his rifle, Thomas levered a hasty shot at the fleeing outlaw. He saw Christie reel and place a hand on his forehead. The tall Indian stumbled the remaining distance to the woods and vanished in the gloom at the base of the trees.

Leaving one posseman with Isbel, Heck and the other two men searched the area quickly, but they found no trace of the Christies. With Isbel's wound demanding immediate attention, the lawmen had no recourse but to withdraw.

Deputy Marshal L. P. Isbel recovered from his wound, but his lawman days were over. His right arm was useless. The whereabouts of the Christies, and the extent of Ned's wound, was not known for some time. Ned's son had received one of Thomas' bullets in a lung, but he recovered. Ned's wound was more serious. The Winchester slug had struck Christie on the bridge of his nose, angling in such a manner that it destroyed his right eyeball. Plunging through the thick bone of the brow, the bullet lodged just above the outlaw's temple. When Christie fell in the high grass at the edge of the woods, Indian friends were lurking in the woods. They dragged him away to safety and to an Indian doctor. The wound healed, but the deep scar on his nose and his sightless right eye were grim reminders to Christie of his experience. He could feel the bullet imbedded in the side of his head by probing with his fingers.

Ned Christie had been a man extremely proud of his dark and fierce good looks. The disfigurement affected him deeply, and he swore a mighty oath to never again speak the English language. As he fought his way back to physical recovery, his entire personality underwent a change. He became vicious, driven by hatred and his iron will to "never leave his beloved hills in the Cherokee Nation."

Ned's storybook attitude may have set a precedent. His lair was in the northern section of the rugged Cookson Hills of eastern Oklahoma, and those hills were to be the bane of lawmen for years to come.

Ned's recuperation took place on a prominent hill scarcely more than a mile south of his homestead site. His tribal friends, nebulous figures never identified by lawmen, constructed a rude wooden shelter on top of the hill. The location was a natural fort. The wooden structure was completely surrounded by huge boulders that were part of an outcropping on the knob of the hill. With horses and crowbars, Ned's friends constructed an impregnable defense post of stone. They kept the wounded outlaw supplied with food and water, and they stood guard. The sentinels, with a splendid view of the surrounding countryside, never did spot signs of unusual activity. The lawmen had learned of the stone fort and they knew that it would require a strong militia to even make the occupants uncomfortable. No attack or foray was ever planned, the deputy marshals had plenty of work cut out for them throughout the Territory, and the site of Ned's stone bastion became known as "Ned Fort Mountain."

The lawmen however, guessed that when Ned's health permitted it, he would begin the work of building a new home. The lawmen's guess was correct, but they were hardly prepared for the type of house that Ned had in mind.

There was an excellent spring at the bottom of a little valley that furnished water for Ned's original house. Instead of utilizing the old site, Christie selected a location on the opposite side of the valley eastward, but just as close to the spring. He had a cellar dug, and planned his construction. Somehow, Christie had managed to acquire a steam engine with an integral boiler, mounted on large cast-iron wheels. He erected a sawmill, and power was furnished

by means of a belt from the power wheel of the steam engine to the saw. An excellent mechanic, Christie easily kept
the rig in repair until the materials for his new house were
cut.

The house was a formidable affair, a log structure of two
stories. The upstairs quarters had slits in lieu of windows
from which a rifle barrel could be thrust, providing a mini-
mum of exposure risk for the shooter. There were no open-
ings at all, other than the door, in the lower portion, and
the walls were constructed with two layers of logs. To
further insure that the fort would be bulletproof, Christie
lined the inside with tough oaken two-by-fours.

Although Ned's friends proved loyal, helping him as much
as they could, they no doubt wondered at the change in
him, and if he truly believed he could make himself safe for
all time from the white man's law.

The white man's law at this time in the Indian Territory
was excellently represented by Deputy Marshal David Vancel Rusk, a man of diminutive stature, five feet four inches,
but known throughout the Nations for his energy and devotion to duty.

Dave Rusk had served as a captain of Company A, First
Battalion, of the Missouri Cavalry, C.S.A. He knew the
topography of the Cherokee Nation well, having engaged
in a number of conflicts in that portion of the Territory, including the Battle of Caving Banks. When the war ended,
Rusk traveled for a number of seasons with the Robinson
Brothers Circus as an exhibition pistol shooter. When Dave
Rusk married, he decided to take on a profession that would
not keep him away from home seasonally. In 1875, he was
sworn in as a deputy marshal in Parker's court.

As the years passed, Rusk accumulated a considerable
stake in the Nations. In 1891, he decided to try his hand
at capturing Ned Christie. He organized a group of
Cherokees he knew to be loyal to the federal government.
The squad surrounded the new Christie house, but as usual,

Christie was ready and waiting. The posse had no sooner arranged itself around the house than Christie's Winchester began to speak. The outlaw's aim was uncanny. In a matter of minutes he had wounded four of the Indian possemen. It was evident by the number of shots coming from the fort that Ned had several confederates.

Just after the fourth posseman was wounded, a weird sound emanated from the Christie building. It was a sound similar to the gobble of a turkey, and the possemen knew that it was the death cry of the Cherokee.

Dave Rusk also knew the meaning of the bloodcurdling cry, and his large black Stetson had twice been pierced with bullets from the fort. Taking stock of his four wounded men, he reluctantly called off the fight. The posse retreated to safe ground.

Later Rusk attempted a lone operation. He scouted the hill country around the Christie, and was startled more than once by the warning whip of a close rifle bullet. Twice, Rusk managed to slip to a point of concealment where he could view Christie's log fort. Each time he was immediately fired upon by the canny Christie. The last encounter resulted in Rusk's new Stetson receiving a bullet hole in the crown.

Dave Rusk sensibly abandoned his one-man attempt, and it was well that he did. Christie knew who it was that persisted in dogging his homesite. Christie sent a slip of paper by an Indian boy into Tahlequah, to be published in the *Cherokee Advocate:*

I thought I saw a big, black potatoe bug in my garden, but it turned out to be the hat of that "little marshal"—Dave Rusk!

Deputy Marshals Heck Bruner and Barney Connelley were another pair of widely known officers in the Territory who tried their hand at capturing the wily Cherokee. With great patience, they crept within view of the fort. Shouted calls brought no response from the house. The two officers then fired into the air as a warning they would start pumping lead into the house. They were not prepared at all for the sudden answer from Christie. A thunderous rifle barrage began, and with leaves and twigs dropping on their heads as bullets cleaved the lawmen's leafy place of concealment, the pair beat a hasty retreat. Ned Christie's fort, they reported, was "well-nigh impregnable."

Ned Christie became a bold figure. He evidently had formed a gang of some sort, but the names of the members were never fully known, at least to the law. The civic-minded Cherokees in the capital town took a dim view of the latest Christie developments, and of the actions of the "cabin gang." The Cherokee Lighthorsemen, due to a lack of "all-out" orders from the tribal government, could not concern themselves with the problem. Christie was wanted by the white man's law. However, they would do what they could when called upon to supplement a federal posse. Generally, the proud Cherokee people looked with dismay upon the growing reputation of Ned Christie.

Dave Rusk had no intention of giving up on the Christie case. As with every deputy marshal in the Territory, he was getting "damned uncomfortable" about the Christie matter. The thought of a lone Indian holding the entire force of Territorial lawmen at bay for four years was a galling thing to contemplate. Rusk was also aware that Christie was "boiling mad" at him.

The federal lawmen worked under the fee system, and the periods of lean income were offset by businesses on the side. Rusk was a merchant, although he had served an apprenticeship as a tailor during his youth. He erected the first brick commercial building in the town of Siloam Springs, Arkansas, to house a hotel. He also owned a general merchandise store in that northwest Arkansas town.

About twenty miles north of Tahlequah, at the little community of Oaks, Rusk had opened a general store. His family was living there, and with the enmity of Christie at a high point, Rusk decided to move his family to the home of a relative in Joplin, Missouri. While he was away, delivering his family, Christie struck.

The Rusk store at Oaks had been left in the charge of William Israel, a Cherokee clerk. Israel was going about his routine duties when a number of horsemen galloped up to the front of the store. All the men, who were Cherokees, dismounted, except one. He was Ned Christie, and he rode his horse right through the front door and into the store building. With a drawn six-shooter he kept the astonished Israel covered while his men ransacked the store. Christie then gestured for the clerk to go out the back door. A partially filled barrel of tar was handy, left over from recent roof repairs on the store building. The bandits proceeded to tar and feather the unfortunate clerk, forcing huge quantities of raw, frontier whiskey down his throat during the process.

Having chased Israel into the woods with a volley of shots, Christie set fire to the store building and ordered his men to mount. They spurred out of the little community, firing their revolvers and whooping loudly.

When Dave Rusk returned, he found his store in ashes and Israel inflamed with a giant hangover, a skin raw from the effects of coal oil used to remove the tar, and burning with indignation.

Rusk was not the only person raging at the depredations of Ned Christie. Many stories of holdups, and the robbing of remote trading posts and stores reached the lawmen. For the most part, witnesses would not, or could not, identify the outlaws. The bandits were reckless Cherokees, however, and that pointed the accusing finger at Ned Christie.

Judge Isaac C. Parker and the United States Marshal at Fort Smith began making plans.

9

PADEN TOLBERT—DEPUTY SHERIFF

Deputy Sheriff Paden Tolbert turned his galloping horse from Railroad Street in a leaning swing to Main Street. He eased the big, black animal to a walk. The wooden sidewalks and the street were jammed with people, some moving along, and others gathered in small groups to pass the time of day. It was 1891, and it was a splendid morning in Clarksville.

As the lawman guided his horse toward the center of town, a bevy of small boys formed, taking advantage of the opening through the throngs made by the man and his mount to trot alongside. They stared in juvenile awe at the Winchester rifle protruding from the saddle boot, its polished walnut stock glistening in the sunlight. The attention of the lads on the other side of the horse was riveted on the ivory-handled Colt .45 peeking from a black leather holster that was suspended from a wide cartridge belt around the lawman's waist. There was admiration in the boys' eyes and a wholesome respect for the law.

Arriving at a cedar hitching rail adjacent to the Main Street water pump and watering trough, Tolbert swung from his saddle with the fluid ease of a veteran horseman. He snapped his reins expertly across the cedar bar, catching and knotting the leather as it looped around the wood. As he pulled his saddlebags from the horse, the lawman glanced at the nearby pump house.

The little round structure sported a high peaked roof with green scalloped shingles. The roof cone was surmounted by a sassy cast-iron weathercock. Inside the pump house were a number of young men the same age as Tolbert. They lounged in awkward casualness against the white circular railing, and instead of the lawman's rough outdoor garb and large hat, they sported stylish brown derbies and shirts of various colors with great, wide vertical stripes. Each young man held the attention of a young lady. The fresh young beauty of the girls was enhanced by white, elaborately lacy styles of dresses.

Swinging the saddlebags across his heavy shoulders, the young deputy sheriff strode through the gateway of the iron lattice fence that encircled the court square.

The village in the valley was proud of the neat, two-story courthouse perched in the exact center of the court square. Atop the brown brick structure was a round white cupola, pointing proudly into the rich blue of the morning sky.

Across from the square, on the east, north, and west sides, were orderly rows of store buildings that presented visored appearances with their porches and awnings. A majority of the buildings were of red brick, but here and there frame structures could be seen. A number of false-fronted saloons blandly faced the street. Tempering the commercial atmosphere of the area were two massive frame residences on the south side of the square, sprouting the gingerbread architectural floss of the era. Between the two houses a large brick Methodist church comfortably nestled its bulk, holding aloft a handsome bell tower.

It was "court day." Throngs of people also filled every corner of the square, and the soft shuffling of hundreds of pairs of boots on the wooden sidewalks over on the streets provided a muted undertone to the hum of many voices. The dirt street was firm and hard from recent showers, and the brilliant morning was not sullied with dust. The air was redolent with the sweet smell of freshly laundered clothing and the gentle fragrance of pipe and cigar smoke.

Deputy Sheriff Paden Tolbert entered the front door of the courthouse, and in the dim, cool interior he sought out the office of the court clerk. That official handed Tolbert a sheet of paper.

"Call 'em in," said the clerk, with a smile.

Tolbert nodded, and, reading the names listed on the sheet, he left the office and climbed the narrow stairs to the second floor.

Out on the square, the buzz of the crowd conversation was punctuated again and again by the shrill calls and laughter of children. Boys in knee pants heckled small girls wearing high-buttoned shoes, and both were dashing pell-mell in and out the crowds of adults.

On the cast-iron railed balcony above the main entrance to the courthouse, the young deputy sheriff appeared. A dozen people sighted him at once, and decline of the crowd noise began.

The lawman on the balcony was a familiar sight. He had the powerful voice necessary for that particular job of the court bailiff. Tolbert tilted his black Stetson to the back of his head and patiently waited. The throngs finally fell silent, and the lawman's big chest swelled. His great voice blared forth:

"E. T. McConnell and T. K. May, Vinson Hamlin and 'Settin-Down' Rhea."

The silence continued a moment. Then, a mighty roar of mirth arose from the crowds, and the horses in the distant wagon yards jerked nervously at their hitches.

James Anderson Rhea, a sheepish grin on his good-natured face, made his way through a gauntlet of shouting friends to the courthouse. Rhea's slight limp was an indication of his painful sciatica, which caused him to sit down at every opportunity.

Bud McConnell shot from the entrance of his drugstore and strode down the wooden walk. Coming abreast of the May store, he paused as the large figure of merchantman T. K. May stepped out of the doorway.

"Did you hear that one?" queried May, as he fell in step with McConnell.

"Hell, yes," snorted Bud, "and so did everybody in Newton County."

"What's all the hurrah about?" The man asking the question peered at his two friends from under the floppy brim of a big, white planter's hat.

McConnell and May halted. The morning sun was climbing higher, and the immaculately dressed May pulled a linen handkerchief from his pocket and dabbed at his white-bearded face. Bud McConnell tilted his Stetson and eyed J. R. Tolbert a moment. Jutting his heavy jaw fiercely, McConnell snapped:

"It's that boy of yours."

Turning to face the courthouse, Bud raised his arm and pointed.

"He's been rhyming off the courthouse porch again!"

The portly Tolbert removed his large hat and scratched his white head, and then he shot a quick glance at McConnell.

"Don't let the old war horse get your goat," laughed May. "He thinks as much of Paden as you do."

"Well, it's too bad you couldn't keep him teaching school," McConnell growled, turning to face the courthouse again so that his twinkling eyes would not belie his rough tone.

"Well," drawled Tolbert, "when he gave up being a disciple of McGuffey, it was because of you and Bud Ledbetter."

"Reckon that will hold you," remarked May.

"Who speaks of Bud Ledbetter," queried a large, raw-

1. Paden Tolbert, 1904. *Courtesy of Stella Tolbert Blackard, Houston, Texas*

2. The early settlers were a hardy breed, living in remote places, fending for themselves, as did the Shroff family—posed here in front of their sod grass house near present-day Afton, Oklahoma. *Courtesy of Everett Shroff, Tulsa, Oklahoma*

3. The remoteness of their dwellings created a problem for many a settler in his relations with outlaws, many of whom he saw more often than the representatives of the law. Dressed in their "Sunday best," the Garth family pose for a picture in front of their lonely log cabin. *Courtesy of Mrs. Sam Sixkiller, Muskogee, Oklahoma*

4. J. R. Tolbert. *Courtesy of Mrs. Gene Tolbert, Clarksville, Arkansas*

5. E. T. "Bud" McConnell, from an engraving. *Courtesy of Mrs. Maud McConnell Poynor, Clarksville, Arkansas*

6. Deputy U.S. Marshal Bud Ledbetter.

7. Johnson County Courthouse, 1876. *Courtesy of Lillian Mickel, Johnson County Historical Association*

8. Judge Isaac Parker, photographed by Mathew Brady in Washington, D.C., 1875, the year the judge took the bench at the Fort Smith Federal Court. *Courtesy the National Archives*

9. The Federal Court, Fort Smith, Arkansas. Judge Parker's courtroom was on the first floor of the building on the right. Adjoining is the jail. *Courtesy Judge Parker Museum, Fort Smith, Arkansas*

10. An exact replica of the famous gallows at Fort Smith.

11. A re-enactment of a late 1890s holdup of the Tahlequah-Fort Gibson stage. *Courtesy Dr. T. L. Ballenger, Tahlequah, Oklahoma*

12. Ned Christie in 1889, published for the first time. *Courtesy Mrs. William Ellis, Wetumka, Oklahoma*

13. Deputy United States Marshal Dan Maples, slain in 1887 by Ned Christie. He was one of sixty-five lawmen of the old Indian Territory killed in action. *Courtesy Beatrice Maple Jones, Bentonville, Arkansas*

14. Deputy United States Marshal Dave Rusk. He pursued Ned Christie for years and finally had the satisfaction of being a member of the posse that trapped the desperado in his lair.

15. Paden Tolbert's posse, 1892, posed by the steam-driven sawmill Christie used to construct his log fort. L. to R.: Becky Polk, Policeman Birkett, Oscar Blackard, Frank Sarber, Vint Gray, Tol Blackard, Mack Peel, Harry Clayless, G. Jefferson, and Paden Tolbert. *Courtesy the McKennon Collection*

16. The end of Ned Christie, Fort Smith Courthouse. *Courtesy the McKennon Collection*

17. The Dynamiters—their skill and bravery destroyed Ned Christie's log fort. L. to R., standing: Bill Smith, Bill Ellis, Paden Tolbert; L. to R., seated: Charley Copeland, G. S. White. *Courtesy Omer Bowman, Seminole, Oklahoma*

18. Wess Bowman, the "beardless youth," with Bill Ellis and John Tolbert, 1892. *Courtesy Stella Tolbert Blackard, Houston, Texas*

19. Bill Cook, leader of the Cook Gang, a dangerous "left-hand draw" man, felt the wrath of Judge Parker.

20. Cherokee Bill after his capture, surrounded by armed lawmen including Deputy U.S. Marshal Bill Smith at extreme right.

21. The Tahlequah-Fort Gibson stage, prime target for the onslaught of the Bill Cook gang. *Courtesy Babe McKnight, Chelsea, Oklahoma*

22. The end of an era—Clarksville's last hanging, 1902. The slayers of Sheriff John Powers are about to hang. On the extreme right, shielding his eyes from the sunlight with a white Stetson, is Bud McConnell. *Courtesy Lillian Mickel, Johnson County Historical Association*

23. Judge Isaac C. Parker, a rare portrait of the "Iron Judge," published for the first time. *Courtesy of Isaac C. Parker, III, Tulsa, Oklahoma*

boned man striding down the walk, his arm linked companionably with a florid-faced fellow who sported a yellowish beard.

"Howdy, Bud," said McConnell, "I see you got Hamlin in tow. Reckon we better get on over to the courtroom."

Lifting their hands in a salute to Tolbert, the four men stepped off the boardwalk and entered the crowd in the street. J. R. Tolbert fished a cheroot from his vest pocket and struck a match. He gazed at the backs of his friends until they were swallowed up in the throng. He laughed aloud as he thought of Paden's "rhyming."

"The boy keeps his sense of humor," mused Tolbert, puffing his cheroot to attain a satisfactory red tip. He thought of the first day he had seen Clarksville.

"Time was," he murmured, "when there just wasn't much laughter in this town."

Tolbert pulled his watch from a pocket and glanced at the time.

"Ten o'clock. The jury is probably impaneled by now. I'll see if Paden is on the witness list this morning."

Deputy Sheriff Paden Tolbert, however, had a manhunt on his hands. Choosing two possemen, the lawman helped them saddle up. Soon, the three men were threading their way along the crowded street until they entered the covered bridge at the east end of Main Street. Clearing the bridge, the horsemen put their mounts into easy gallops and topped East Hill. Within minutes they were traveling northward, and at dusk they overtook their quarry on top of Ozone Mountain.

From his concealment of a clump of second growth cedar trees, Deputy Sheriff Paden Tolbert eyed a white-haired old lady. She had just left her weather-beaten house, carrying a bucket, and she was approaching a well, not three feet from Tolbert's evergreen shield. She set her bucket on the rough boards of the well box and began uncoiling the frayed draw rope from its wooden peg.

"Beg pahdon, ma'am," Tolbert whispered, the soft tones accentuating his Georgia brogue, "ah'm the law from Clarksville. Please, just act natural like, whilst I talk to you."

Startled, the old lady's toothless gums clamped down on her generous pinch of Garrett's. She shot a searching glance in Tolbert's direction. Seeing his face through the network of young evergreen boughs, she quickly regained her composure and allowed a wooden well bucket to slowly descend in the well. A cast-iron pulley, crudely wired to the weather-cracked crossbeam of the well structure, squealed in unoiled protest.

"What do ye want of me?" Her voice was a hoarse croak.

"That man that rode up here an hour ago. His name is Yates. We trailed him from Clarksville, and we're taking him back on a charge of horse stealing."

The mountain woman was not one to remain rattled for long.

"Jee-ho-sephat," she whispered, "he told me he was a drummer name of Smith, headed for Harrison town. He gimme fifty cents to feed him a bite and fer a place to sleep tonight."

"What part of the house is he in?"

"He's in the bedroom, on the west side. He's probably hauling his boots off by now."

"You just stay here by the well, ma'am," Tolbert instructed.

Motioning to his brother John, and Wesley Bowman, who were crouched nearby, Tolbert quietly retreated a distance into the dense forest that surrounded the house. When his companions appeared, Tolbert outlined a plan.

"Wess, you take the back door, just ease it open and slip in. John and I will take the front door."

With the ease of long practice, the three young men walked quickly to their places. Bowman gingerly lifted the latch on the back door and stepped quickly into the kitchen. Arriving at the front door, Paden and John, taking long,

tiptoe strides in order to soften the tread of their heavy
boots, slipped inside. They met Bowman in the shabby
parlor—three dim figures with drawn six-shooters, in the
gloom of falling dusk.

The only room unexplored was behind a closed door that
hid the bedroom from view.

Motioning to Bowman and his brother to stand clear,
Tolbert raised a heavy boot and sent the door crashing in-
ward. Taking a long stride with his momentum, Tolbert entered the room and came face to face with Yates, who was
seated on a bed. In an instant Yates snatched up a Colt
that lay at his side on the quilt. Without pausing in his
stride, Tolbert again launched out with his booted foot and
caught the revolver squarely, sending it clattering to a corner
of the room. Yates submitted meekly to the heavy iron
manacles Tolbert clamped on his wrists.

"You are riding that fine mare you stole back to Clarksville," Tolbert said, motioning the slumped figure on the bed
to pull on his boots.

Darkness had come, and the sky was streaked with flashes
of lightning. A spring storm was brewing, and heavy thunder echoed across the mountain top.

"Old 'tater wagon is a-rumbling, heading for the barn,"
observed Bowman, leading three horses from the forest.

John Tolbert led the stolen mare from a rickety barn, and
the three lawmen saddled her. The handcuffed Yates was
ordered to mount. Rain began to fall as the four horsemen
left the house in the Ozark Mountains and began a soggy
ride southward to Clarksville.

The next day Paden Tolbert emerged from the post office
and crossed the street to the square, to be accosted by Ab
Allen, the tall, raw-boned son of the local blacksmith and
wagon maker.

"Pretty good job of trailing Yates," Allen said, a woebe-
gone expression on his lean face.

Paden laughed. "Well, now. He sho' won't be the last one."

Allen snorted. "He just might be the last critter you'll chase as a deputy sheriff."

Allen was referring to Paden's project of applying for a commission as deputy marshal in the Federal Western District of Arkansas.

"It takes time," Paden said. "They check your record pretty good."

Allen nodded. He was a schoolteacher during the winter months when his father's smithy and wagon trade slackened, but the past year had witnessed him often as a posseman. Posse work, however, was becoming sporadic. The last really big case in Johnson County was the Jim Holland affair, as far as Allen was concerned. Holland escaped jail and was trailed by the "two invincibles" of Johnson County—Bud Ledbetter and John Powers. Ledbetter and Powers had indeed established some sort of a record, they trailed Holland on horseback for twenty-eight days—clear to Tennessee.

The slender form of Wess Bowman appeared on the front steps of the courthouse. Sighting his friends, he strolled in their direction, casually tucking a few bills of green currency into a shirt pocket.

"Well, there is a little bit of law work left for the lucky ones," sighed Allen, dramatically spreading his arms.

"Not luck, just pluck," answered Bowman cockily.

Tolbert laughed. He pulled a letter from his pocket.

"You boys might be interested to know that Jacob Yoes, the Marshal at Fort Smith, has your applications—with my letter of recommendation. I just picked this up in the morning mail."

With eagerness, Bowman and Allen read the letter, and they knew they were under consideration by the authorities at Fort Smith.

"How about your own application, heard anymore about it?" Allen asked, handing the letter back to Tolbert.

"Nope," replied Paden, "but I will be notified when to take the oath of office."

"Well, we're beholden to you for your help," said Bowman sincerely.

"I never would have been in line for an appointment either, without recommendations," Tolbert remarked.

Paden Tolbert was extremely proud of the two young men he had trained. Bowman still had a couple of months to go before his twenty-first birthday, and when he had approached Tolbert two years before to apply for posse duty, he would not have appeared unusual if he had been dressed in knee pants. Even now, his slight build and boyish face completely belied his growing skill as a lawman. Paden had interrogated the youth in the same manner he had observed Bud McConnell use so many times. Tolbert was impressed by the straightforwardness of Bowman, and began the training process, good-naturedly absorbing the double-headed puns of being partial to "schoolboys."

The courthouse boys did not kid and joke about young Bowman for long. The slender lawman had a rare mixture of tenderness and wildcat. One day on the square, he risked bitten fingers in removing a tin can that was tied to the tail of a mongrel dog. Then Bowman sailed into a rowdy, drunken bully who had been bedeviling the dog for laughs. Bowman was outweighed by fifty pounds, but bystanders had to pull him off the yelping fellow.

Tolbert left his two friends animatedly discussing their prospects of becoming federal lawmen, and returned to the post office.

"Just finished the sorting," the postmaster said, "I knew I saw a package for you."

He handed Tolbert a thick, rectangular package. Tucking his package under his arm, Paden strolled back to the court square. The warm spring sunshine, brilliant after the rain the night before, bathed him with mild warmth.

Crossing his arms, and leaning against one of the several

small shade trees that a civic group had set out a decade
ago, Tolbert paused, contentedly scanning the groups of
townspeople passing to and fro on the boardwalks across the
street. He did not have long to wait.

Charley "Chark" Pennington and Ed Connelley stepped
out of Bud McConnell's drugstore, and Paden hailed them.
They crossed the street to the square.

"You got 'em," said Pennington, eying the package.

"Yep," answered Paden, "and the Fort Smith printers did
an elegant job."

Tolbert tore open one end of the package and extracted
a sheet. It was a handbill, printed with red ink.

"COME ONE—COME ALL," the colorful poster read,
"VIEW the scientific MARVEL of the AGES—PROFES-
SOR Gander will demonstrate the art of FLYING by a
death-defying FLIGHT from the TOP of the Johnson
County COURT HOUSE Saturday!"

The young men nodded their approval, and Ed Connelley displayed a thin roll of handbills.

"Here's all that is left of a batch Chark had printed. Will
Mitchell has gone down the Cabin Creek road with some,
and John Swaggerty plans to leave about noon with the rest
of the bills for Coal Hill."

"Here comes Ben," Tolbert said.

"Howdy, Paden," said Ben Pennington as he walked up
to the group. "How is it going?"

"We got the county pretty well covered," Paden answered. "How about the newspaper?"

"The announcement was run last week, and it will be
in this week's issue, too."

"Well, then," said Paden, "I'll see you all Saturday."

When Saturday came, the Clarksville merchants began
to get excited as hordes of people descended upon the
village to witness Professor Gander's flight. Many merchants hastily hired additional clerks to accommodate their
jammed stores. Folks from the surrounding counties of

Franklin, Pope, Newton, and Yell were swarming the court square and every foot of the streets. Practically the entire population of Johnson County was in town before the noon hour came. The old town pump that was as dependable as the sunrise, began to wane from the steady demand put upon it. It was the biggest crowd ever to assemble in the history of Clarksville.

The town's four wagon yards were hopelessly bulging, and wagons and buggies of all descriptions were nestled under convenient shade trees, or clustered in open lots at the edges of the residential sections. The railroad station was witnessing an unusual discharge of passengers.

A group of students from the Arkansas Industrial College at Fayetteville had arrived. They had convinced the headmaster that a scientific feat such as proposed by Professor Gander should be witnessed by students. Their arrival in town created a rumor that Gander was from the big college, and not from Clarksville's own newly established Arkansas Cumberland College as had been assumed by many.

"Well, it makes little difference," extolled one merchant to his customers. "In a *college* town, you can just naturally expect to see new-fangled things going on."

Everyone maintained a sharp lookout in the humanity-jammed streets for a tall man of academic appearance. Surely he would be wearing a stovepipe hat, and he would necessarily be a man of slight build.

As the hour of one o'clock neared, the court square became a solid, inpenetrable block of humanity. In the streets, even pedestrians could scarcely squirm their way along.

The announced hour of flight arrived. Someone began tolling the big bell in the tower of the Methodist church. All eyes that could see the spot were riveted on the iron-railed balcony that surmounted the front porch of the Johnson County courthouse.

No one uptown bothered to notice the sudden rumble of a farm wagon entering the covered bridge. A farmer in the foothills of the Ozark Mountains had been plowing in a rocky field near the Ozone road. A passing horseman had handed him a poster, but he had not bothered to read it until that morning.

"Pack a lunch, maw," he bellowed at his wife, "whilst I corral the young'uns. Some dern-fool teacher is a-going to jump offen the top of the courthouse and kill hisself!"

The farmer was forced to halt his wagon when the vehicle emerged from the bridge. It was impossible to find even a pathway through the throngs in the street. Despite his late arrival, though, it turned out that the farmer was to have a vantage view.

Thousands of straining eyes were on the courthouse, and a movement was seen, but it was not on the porch balcony. A series of rectangular windows circumvented the cupola that reared high above the roof of the building. The windows around the cupola were heavy—with horizontal wood louvres—and neatly painted white. The window facing Main Street was slowly pushed to one side. There were gasps from the crowd—the man was more daring than anyone thought. He had picked the cupola, which was much higher than the porch. A roar of hand-clapping applause arose from the admiring crowd. The window was edged a little farther open, and the enormous crowd held its breath. A dead silence prevailed.

Presently, an arm appeared, thrusting out a large, white object. Startled shouts rose from the street as an alarming drumming sound was heard, and the white object suddenly soared out over Main Street.

It was a huge white goose, in frightened flight!

The big bird wobbled high overhead, and then veered eastward. Directly over Main Street, it made an uncertain flight as far as the covered bridge, where it accomplished an ungainly landing on the ridge pole of the roof.

Professor Gander had flown.

It took the remaining summer months of 1891 for Clarksville to recover from the aerial antics of Professor Gander. Most of the crowd on that memorable Saturday had left town abruptly—and there was much red-faced anger extant. An enterprising lad had invested in a carton of the old standby encourager for laying hens, realistic white glass eggs. Although there had been a rush demand for his loudly hawked "soo-vee-neers," he suddenly had to drop his still partially filled box of fragile merchandise and flee from his erstwhile customers until he lost himself in the crowds.

As time can become a balm for wounded feelings, Clarksville's anger eventually gave way to belly laughs. The plotters of the famed flight made certain that their complicity in the affair was not known for many years. The unprecedented "success" of the event resulted in many persons claiming to have had a hand in it. Those factors served to aid the true originators in their understandable desire to remain incognito, and Professor Gander became a legend in Johnson County.

Other than bearing out Bud McConnell's prediction of Paden Tolbert's sense of humor, the Gander incident marked the end of Tolbert's leisure time as he became a deputy United States marshal in the Indian Territory.

10

PADEN TOLBERT—DEPUTY MARSHAL

"It sounds like the boys 'shooting anvils' on Christmas Eve," commented Deputy Marshal Dave Rusk, who was perched on his haunches like a contented, feeding squirrel.

A well-tailored deputy marshal wearing a stylish dark gray suit that matched his pearl gray Stetson eyed his fellow officer with a puzzled look. The two lawmen were busily discussing Federal Judge Isaac C. Parker, whose deep-pitched voice could be heard like the tolling of a distant, enormous bell.

Deputy Marshal G. S. White toyed with his enormous graying mustache for a moment. Unable to restrain his curiosity, the tall, slender officer was forced to admit his unfamiliarity with some of the local customs.

"What has Judge Parker's voice got to do with an anvil? And for that matter, why would anybody want to shoot at an anvil?" Using a twig, Rusk was idly scratching designs on the smooth, bare earth that constituted the grounds of the United States Court at Fort Smith. The two men were a short distance from the steps that led up to a front porch of the big building. It was a mild mid-September afternoon in 1891, and the windows of the courtroom on the first floor were open. Court was in session, and the powerful voice of Judge Parker was bearing down on important facts of law.

Pausing in his earthen art work, Rusk peered up from underneath his shaggy, white eyebrows.

"Kinda new in these parts, aintcha, bub?"

White laughed. "I come from down in Tennessee, bub."

"It's like this. On celebrating days, such as the Fourth of July or Christmas Eve, boys hereabouts will get hold of a pair of big anvils. They'll tamp the hardy hole of one full of gunpowder and heft the other one upside down on top of it. Then they'll touch off the powder with a long, burning stick. She just jars the ground something awful when she goes off. You can sort of feel it instead of hearing it, a long ways off."

White listened to the sound of Judge Parker's distant, deep-bass voice.

"Reckon you are right. I do seem to feel the sound of his voice."

"The judge is pretty angry today; that is Shep Busby on trial in there."

White nodded. The month before, Busby had slain Deputy Marshal Barney Connelley in the Nations.

"He'll hang, just as sure as green apples will cramp you," Rusk muttered.

A heavy-set young man crossing the court grounds caught the attention of the lawmen. Noticing that he was observed, the stranger paused.

"I beg your pahdon, gentlemen," he asked, "is the court still in session?"

"It sure is," replied White, "but I think it will break up soon. The judge has been charging the jury for over an hour."

"Thank you, suh." The man's voice flowed like warmed honey into a thin china bowl; it was rich with the slurred brogue of the Deep South.

Rusk eyed the black Stetson, bronzed face, and polished, heavy-duty boots of the newcomer.

"Are you one of the laws here?"

"Well, no," drawled the stranger, "but I reckon ah will be after today."

Courteously taking leave of the lawmen, Paden Tolbert walked away toward the porch steps.

Paden Tolbert climbed the steps of the big porch. There was a scraping of chair legs on the floor inside and a rising hum of conversation. Court had been adjourned.

Tolbert stepped over to the railing of the porch as the screen door popped open and groups of men began pouring out into the late afternoon sunlight. Waiting for the jam to thin out, Tolbert extracted a letter from his coat pocket. Unfolding the paper, he slowly read the contents—for the tenth time. It was his long awaited notice to appear in Fort Smith for the oath of office, and his commission as deputy United States marshal in the Western District of Arkansas.

Paden Tolbert's project to enter federal service had progressed smoothly. John Sarber, former marshal at Fort Smith, had supplemented letters of recommendation supplied by Sheriffs Bud McConnell and W. S. Jett. The excellent references had no doubt speeded up the consideration process, but to Tolbert, the summer, since the flight of Professor Gander, had seemed to drag endlessly.

Tolbert was not a stranger entirely to Fort Smith. A number of times when Bud McConnell had wanted to sit in on a particularly interesting case, he had invited his friend to accompany him. The famous judge, with now snow white hair and beard, fascinated Tolbert. No one in the courtroom ever had to strain his ears to hear the remarks of the big judge. His stentorian voice was as powerful and positive as his actions and his news-making decisions. Although he was totally unlike him in appearance, much about Judge Parker reminded Tolbert of Bud McConnell. Both men were strong-willed, and both were convinced that law and order could prevail, and should exist in all communities. Remoteness of locale or a confused conception of law enforcement was no excuse for anti-social behavior, was the creed of both men.

The crowd soon passed through the door, and Tolbert entered the cool, dim hall. He saw the sign above a door: U. S. MARSHAL AND COURT CLERK. Entering the door, Tolbert faced two large men seated by a huge rolltop desk. Introducing himself, Tolbert handed over his letter. Marshal Jacob Yoes came to his feet and shook Tolbert's hand warmly.

"Glad to see you, sir. And I want you to meet Judge Parker of the United States Court."

The judge rose and shook Tolbert's hand.

"Well, sir. The marshal and I have gone over your record. I might add, it is a very good one."

Marshal Yoes handed the pleased Tolbert a small sheet of paper.

"This is the oath of office that you will sign."

With abruptness, but with his eyes twinkling, Judge Parker picked up a large Bible from the desk.

"Wheeler, the court clerk, is still over in the courtroom arranging his notes. Do you suppose I have enough authority to administer the oath?"

Tolbert laughed. The rumors he had heard about the big man were true. Aloof, and businesslike to the point of coldness with deputy marshals during courtroom sessions, the judge was a kindly man and a possessor of a sparkling sense of humor off the bench. The judge's personal interest in his lawmen was a legend among the men of the force.

"I have met you before, sir."

"I remember the meeting very well, young man. You had a touch of the asthma the day I met you."

Tolbert laughed again.

"And now, if you will raise your right hand, I will swear you in."

Jacob Yoes filled out the commission form and handed it to Tolbert.

"Wheeler has already signed this."

Judge Parker extracted a large pen from the ink well on the desk, and with his quick, flourishing penmanship that usually was illegible, he signed the oath of office form.

"And now, young man, if you will excuse me, I must hurry home. We finished the session today rather early. Mary will be glad to see me in the daylight, for a change."

Jacob Yoes glanced out the hall door. The shadows were darkening.

"Judge, you had better hurry."

With the departure of the judge, Marshal Yoes handed Tolbert the rules and regulations booklet for deputy marshals.

"This is something for you to read. As I mentioned in my letter to you, it will be about a week before the deputy will be available that I want you to train with. It is a custom that we have found to be very good."

Jacob Yoes opened a drawer of the desk and took out a silver badge.

"This badge, sir, belongs to you."

Paden Tolbert was considerably impressed again by his meeting with Judge Parker and the man who was now his boss. Along with the pleasure of being accepted into federal service was the sense of duty that accompanied the job.

The transition from a peaceful town to a lawless, frontier country would have appalled a lawman without the rigid training that was Tolbert's Johnson County heritage. The quiet man with the rich southern brogue, was accepted quickly by the keen-eyed veteran lawmen at the headquarters in Fort Smith, although Tolbert was not fully aware of the fact at first.

Marshal Jacob Yoes conducted Tolbert on a tour to meet the various officials of the court. The deputy marshals who were not on duty at the moment were also introduced.

"Tolbert," announced the marshal, "I want you to work with "Cap" White for a while."

Tall, dignified Gideon S. "Cap" White had a very definite military set to his ship-mast back. He had served as a captain in the Union Cavalry during the war. He came from a home in Tennessee that mirrored a typical drama that occurred in many homes in the South. White's father was a native of New York State, and was strong in his belief that the "North was right," while his mother was an equally positive-minded person who was convinced the "cause" was right. It was a home of split allegiance, and White elected to side with his father.

"Tolbert," said White, acknowledging the introduction to the Johnson County man, "I can tell by your speech that you would have been a Johnny Reb if you had been old enough to shoulder a Springfield."

"The war has been over for twenty-six years," calmly replied Tolbert.

White's huge, gray mustache quivered slightly as a grin crinkled his sharp eyes. A man of positive likes and dislikes, White believed in finding out the nature of a man right away.

"True," agreed White. "By the way, they still call me 'Captain'—I was ranked as such in the Union Cavalry for four years."

"Well," said Tolbert, "I am happy that you were able to survive your right to fight for what you believed in."

White laughed. He believed he was going to take a liking for the serious young deputy marshal.

Leaving the court building, the two men walked to the business district of Fort Smith. Garrison Avenue, the wide main thoroughfare, was well filled with wagon and horse traffic. Rows of brick store buildings testified that Fort Smith had prospered commercially during the years Judge Parker had been on the bench. McKibben's Saloon attracted the two men. Entering the establishment, they ordered up mugs of foamy Lemp's beer. They discovered that each had spent considerable time teaching school.

"And, you say your father is an old hand with a newspaper," queried White, delicately wiping away a bit of foam from his big mustache. "I edited a newspaper in West Fork, *The Republican*, I am a member of that party, you know."

Tolbert laughed. He was forming a liking for the tall, spare marshal.

"I'll tell you how I got started in law work," offered White, signaling the barkeeper for two more beers. "I drifted out to Abilene, up in Kansas, when the war ended. I was in a saloon when the town marshal, Wild Bill Hickok, came in. There was a bunch of men in there, all tanked up, shouting about how they were going to take the town apart.

"I was just a bystander, and after Hickok had cleaned the place out, he offered to buy me a drink. Well, I accepted, and talked with Bill Hickok for a while. Abilene was a tough trail's-end town in those days, and while there were mostly men in town, there were some women and children. You can't just let the tough bunch have free rein. Hickok was practically by himself on his job, and there are just a hell of a lot of men who resent one man telling them how to behave. The job took a lot of pure courage.

"Hickok's job got me to thinking. It seemed to me that a rough town, or territory, had to have men who were willing to take risks to have law and order established. Now, that's a worthwhile profession, and I thought about it a long time. Hickok had a mustache—as big as mine is now—and that is where I got the idea of growing it. I really admired Hickok's nerve.

"I figured that a young fellow should get into a useful line of work as soon as possible, since the war was over. I moved on down to West Fork, Arkansas, and taught school quite a bit there. Of course, you can't be in this country long without hearing about Judge Parker. I just came down here and announced that I could do some good in the Territory."

As the days passed, Tolbert found that the warrants he and White were given had only to do with whiskey peddlers.

"Don't ever underestimate a whiskey peddler," White explained, sensing Tolbert's disappointment. "It is a felony to sell whiskey to the Indians, but it is not the kind of a charge that most men would be willing to get into a shoot-out over. They come along peacefully enough once you catch them, but there is always that exception that a lawman must watch for at all times—if he intends to stay alive."

Observing Tolbert's interest, White continued:

"One of the best examples is the time, back in '87, when Deputy Marshal Phillips arrested Seaborn Kalijah for whiskey selling. Phillips had three possemen with him, and before they could break camp and start for Fort Smith with their prisoner, Phillips got word to report in Eufaula on another case.

"Eufaula was not far away, so Phillips put his possemen in charge and left.

"When Phillips returned the next day, he found his three possemen dead. Two had been chopped up with an ax, and their bodies piled on the big campfire. The bodies were half burned up. The third posseman had been shot, but the whiskey peddler had used the ax on the body, too. It was hacked almost beyond recognition.

"Well, Phillips set out after Kalijah, and it did not take him long to track the killer down. However, it was long enough for Phillips to cool down some, but just the same Kalijah knew that he was in danger of getting his head blown off. He was meek as a lamb on the trip to Fort Smith. Judge Parker took care of Kalijah!"

Tolbert knew that he was learning good, practical lessons. Also, the trips into the field were good experience. Tolbert was quick to learn that, in most cases, the lawmen were forced to do their own tracking. Most citizens in the Territory would just as soon not be asked questions about wanted men.

White explained another factor.

"The law is getting complicated, Tolbert. Time was when you had an assignment to bring a man in, you brought him in, and that ended your job. Now, they are getting some crackajack lawyers in court, all you can hear is 'evidence.' We have to learn to jot down names of witnesses, if there are any, and to pick up anything that can be used as evidence. You'll be surprised how many times you have to appear in court to testify."

Tolbert and White stepped out on the porch of the court building one morning. It was winter, and a dreary, slow sleet storm was in progress. Cap White was riffling a stack of warrants with his lean, long fingers.

"Jehosephat," he exclaimed. "These warrants will take us all over the Nations. So far, we have had good luck. We could just hop a train over in the Territory, and get pretty close to where we were going to work. With this batch here, we are going to have to take a wagon. We'll hire us a cook, and we'll outfit for a couple of weeks."

Watching the falling sleet for a minute, White observed: "And we better get us some woolly coats."

As the months passed, Paden Tolbert graduated to top assignments, his apprenticeship behind him. He had learned a valuable lesson. Even the lowly whiskey peddler would understandably object to a trip to Fort Smith. Facing the criminal element in the Territory required a quick estimate of a man on the part of the lawman. Would the man fight, or sullenly submit and hope for a chance to escape before the doors of the Fort Smith jail clanged shut.

"In a way," White explained one day, "Judge Parker put a lot of fight into those critters, but it sure makes the job a lot more satisfactory to know that if you can get your man to Fort Smith, the law will take care of him."

Although his spare time was now occupied with courting a beautiful lass he had met in the Territory, Tolbert was pleased to see his friends. Ab Allen and Wess Bowman, were sworn into federal service. Again, Bowman's deceiving youthful appearance had brought questions, but Tolbert satisfied Marshal Yoes with a simple statement: "I'll call for that fellow to stride a horse in my posse for any job in the Territory you want to name."

Tolbert began receiving his share of lonely assignments. There were never enough lawmen on hand at Fort Smith to permit multiple assignments on every case. As he traveled the lonely reaches of the Indian Nations with only the creaking of saddle leather for company, he often thought about Johnson County. His father was a happy man, even in spite of Paden's brother, John, who had also joined the ranks of deputy marshals. J. R. Tolbert would have peaches that spring, and if his faith in the county's soil and climate was justified, the Elbertas would be as large as though they had been nourished by Georgia loam. Tolbert admired his father's pluck, for many old-timers had assured the ex-Georgian that even if his trees brought forth buds, the unpredictable Arkansas spring would nip them with a sudden freeze. The '91 crop had suffered a setback.

But, it was good to know that the people of Johnson County were concerned with subjects about the weather and crops, instead of lawlessness. The faith that rigid law enforcement could some day tame the savage Territory provided a comfortable, silent companion for Tolbert.

Meeting Cap White on New Year's Day in Fort Smith, Tolbert mentioned an outstanding fact for the year 1891 which had just passed.

"There has been only one hanging this year."

"Yes," replied White, "it has been a mild year for the old gallows, but not for the court. The only man hung was

Bood Crumpton, last June—before you came on the force. But there are a lot of birds on the scout that sooner or later will have to answer to the judge. Sheppard Busby, the man that killed Barney Connelley, will stretch rope in '92. So don't let that slow gallows year fool you. This country is a hell of a long ways from being settled. That Dalton bunch up in Kansas will bear watching. I know a couple of those boys, used to be on the force here. Now that they are on the scout, there is going to be real trouble. Henry Starr is one Cherokee that is going to turn into a bad one. There is another Cherokee—a full blood—over in the Cookson Hills, that killed a marshal back in '87. He is still on the loose."

Paden Tolbert wondered if he would be in on the kill of one of those headline desperadoes. Warrants for all of them were plentiful, but with discouraging regularity, the lawmen were unable to track down the nimble wolves.

"The wolf of the Cookson Hills," however, was a different proposition. His lair was well known to the lawmen. On October 11, 1892, another attacking party had formed at the site of Ned Christie's fort. The group had organized quietly, and then ridden posthaste to Christie's place. As usual, the element of surprise was not with the attackers, Ned was well prepared to receive visitors.

The lawmen called for a surrender and received the customary hail of lead for an answer, and the volley had a lethal effect. Comprising the attacking force were deputy marshals Dave Rusk, Charley Copeland, Milo Creekmore, D. C. Dye; and aiding were Joe Bowers and John Fields. Bowers received a bullet in his ankle and Fields was struck in the neck.

Reorganizing, the angered lawmen called for Christie to send out any women and children that might be in the building. Somewhat to their surprise, two women and a child appeared at the door. They were conducted to a safe place. Knowing the futility of pouring lead into the ponderous building, the lawmen cast about for some means to effect a penetration of Ned's defense.

The ground surrounding the fort had been carefully gleaned of bushes, saplings, and large stones that could offer concealment to the attackers. An outbuilding stood a distance from the fort, near the fringe of the woods. Eying the cleared ground, the lawmen decided to utilize the smooth area to their advantage. An old farm wagon, used by the outlaw to haul lumber from his sawmill during the construction of the fort, was standing nearby. The lawmen dragged the wagon back to the safety of the woods. Scouring the forest, they gathered material, piling dried leaves, twigs, and straw into the wagon bed. Then they set the load afire, and many strong backs gave the vehicle a mighty shove.

Trailing sparks and smoke, the wagon sped out into the clearing, but groans of dismay went up as it struck the outbuilding a glancing blow—spilling the fiery load. The wagon, listlessly dragging a broken sideboard, rolled a short distance beyond the outhouse and came to a halt. However, burning debris had tumbled against a wall of the outhouse, and the small structure began to burn. The lawmen were not cheered by this unexpected conflagration. Christie had learned his lesson well—the outhouse was located too far from the fort to endanger it. Watching the outhouse burn in futile fury, the lawmen heard Christie's Cherokee death cry, the weird gobbling sound already portrayed death.

Charley Copeland attempted a "bombing." He wired a number of dynamite sticks together and fixed a fuse. It was quite a distance across the clearing for a man to throw an object, but Copeland tried. He wound up and put every ounce of effort from his powerful shoulders into a tremendous pitch. The bomb, with fuse sputtering, sailed across the clearing and bounced off a wall of the fort. The fuse, knocked loose by the impact, sizzled merrily on the ground until it exhausted itself. The lawmen were checked.

A hasty consultation was held, and Deputy Marshal Creekmore leaped on his horse and pounded away toward Tahlequah. He sent a telegram to Marshal Yoes in Fort Smith:

"SEND DEPUTIES TO NED CHRISTIE'S AT ONCE. WE HAVE SUR-ROUNDED HIM BUT HAVE NOT ENOUGH MEN. JOHN FIELDS AND JOE BOWERS, OF OUR PARTY, ARE SHOT. FIELDS WILL DIE."

Marshal Yoes answered immediately:

"HAVE WIRED EVERYWHERE FOR DEPUTIES. YOU WILL HAVE LOTS OF HELP TONIGHT. HOLD THE FORT BY ALL MEANS AND GET THEM THIS TIME."

Creekmore then sought the aid of the city marshal of Tahlequah. That night there was a force of thirty men around the Christie fort. It was rumored that Christie had three confederates, possibly more, in the fort. They were said to be Bearpaw, Walk-About, and Peek-Above.

However, the large posse failed to intimidate the Cherokee outlaw; he sounded his gobble and then let loose a blistering volley of lead. And the lawmen sought cover fast. From concealment, the lawmen brought every rifle and pistol into play. It was a furious fusillade, but the target could just as well have been a stone mountain. No damage what-soever was incurred by Ned's fort.

It was quiet in the area after the guns ceased hammering. As the disgusted lawmen retreated, they could hear Ned's fierce gobbling.

11

TO THE WOLF'S LAIR

Deputy Marshal Wess Bowman, his slender figure erect with eagerness, buttonholed Paden Tolbert on the streets of Fort Smith.

"How about joining up, Paden?"

His mind concentrating on a current assignment, Tolbert halted and looked quizzically for a moment at Bowman. He tilted his Stetson to the back of his head, and then the reason for Bowman's eager question dawned on him.

That morning Chief Marshal Jacob Yoes had summoned Tolbert to the Federal building, and he acquainted his deputy marshal with a plan that had very much to do with the current event Fort Smith was buzzing about—the defiance of Ned Christie. October 1892 was drawing to a close, and the big marshal had been a busy man since the last abortive attempt, the eleventh of the month, on Ned Christie's fort.

"Tolbert," the marshal had boomed. "I am placing you in charge of an all-out effort to bring in Ned Christie!"

After discussing details of the coming project, Tolbert left the Federal building and was walking along a street when Bowman had stopped him. Bowman repeated his question:

"Come on, now, how about joining up?"

Tolbert eyed his friend, and then he pretended to tug thoughtfully at his thick mustache so that his hand would hide his grin.

"Well, now, Wess," he drawled, "you don't need my permission to join the Army, but it moved out of Fort Smith years ago."

Tolbert laughed and slapped his friend on the back.

"We just got time to catch the 'dinky' for Clarksville, though it beats me how you found out so soon."

The pleased Bowman fell into step with Tolbert, and the two young men headed for the railroad depot.

"Possemen from Clarksville, eh?" Bowman asked.

"Yep," said Tolbert, "the marshal agreed that I should pick my posse."

Arriving in Clarksville, the two deputy marshals set up headquarters in the courthouse. The crowd of loafers on the court square was no larger than usual, and Tolbert guessed that his project was still relatively unknown.

Soon dusk came, and Sheriff John Powers climbed upon a chair and set a match to the big lamp that hung from the ceiling of his office. Several men arrived as the dusk outside changed to darkness. Tolbert addressed the gathering:

"Men, our office has an important job to do, and we need possemen; that is why I sent for you. There is a heavy reward now on Ned Christie, and I got orders to bring him in. He is extremely dangerous, and he is a dead shot, and he probably won't give up. He has built a regular fort in the Nations, near Tahlequah, and he has some sort of a gang. We don't know how many. We'll leave first thing in the morning and join a bunch in Fort Smith. I have my brother, John, taking care of that end. Then, we'll take a train for West Fork, and from there we'll go overland by wagon and horses to the Going Snake District of the Cherokee Nation, about twelve–thirteen miles this side of Tahlequah. It is going to be a tough, dangerous job. What do you say?"

It was a long speech for Tolbert. The group knew the former deputy sheriff well, and they knew that it was indeed an important event to elicit so many studied words. Every man in the group nodded his assent.

Tolbert smiled slightly. The ready acceptance came as no surprise to him.

One of the group was a tall, raw-boned Negro, Frank Polk, with the improbable nickname of Becky.

"Becky here, will do the cooking," Tolbert explained. "We don't know how long this job will take, and we don't aim to go hungry."

Becky grinned his delight. Posse work was an old story to him. An excellent cook, he was a veteran of many Johnson County excursions with lawmen, and on weekend outings with addicts of the town's favorite sport—fishing trips on Big Piney Creek. Tolbert also knew that Becky could handle firearms with coolness and accuracy.

Taking his notebook from his pocket, Tolbert entered the names of the posse, and then formally swore them in. He eyed one new lawman with a grin.

"Sarber," he said, "you won't be the youngest feller on this outing, Harry Clayland of Fort Smith is on the list, and he is just seventeen."

Young Frank Sarber laughed. He was a highly pleased man. At eighteen, he was delighted at the chance for adventure in the Territory, where his father, John Sarber, had served as marshal in the early seventies.

Tolbert addressed the group:

"You men will have the job of rear guard. Christie is a slippery feller, if he gets through the first line, we want to stop him before he gets loose in the woods. You won't actually need rifles. I'd rather see you pack shotguns and pistols. Suit yourselves, though. Sheriff Powers will loan guns to those who don't have them."

Crowding around the sheriff's gun rack were Vint Gray, a tall man, and two shorter though heavier figures—Tol and Oscar Blackard. They selected their firearms.

Tucking his notebook in a pocket, Tolbert turned to Bowman.

"Wess, you take charge; have the men at the depot a little

before train time in the morning. I am going to borrow a horse and spend the night at Ludwig, with the folks."

"Give my regards to Lucy," Bowman called after the departing Tolbert.

After he had been sworn in the year before, Tolbert met Lucy Rose Turner, the daughter of Truss Turner of Muldrow, a small town in the Territory ten miles west of Fort Smith. After a short courtship, Tolbert married the pretty nineteen-year-old girl. He had taken his bride to the home of his father until such time as he could afford to buy a house. Tolbert's sister Maggie was only two years younger than Lucy, and the two young ladies took a delight in helping care for Stella, the deputy marshal's nine-year-old sister. With the exception of David, who was twelve, Tolbert's brothers were old enough to be away from home with affairs of business. J. R. Tolbert could not resist a pun when he was introduced to his new daughter-in-law:

"I have lost a son, but by jupiter-creekers, at last I have got a peach!"

Before leaving Clarksville, the deputy marshals asked the telegrapher to monitor any news concerning the posse. Tolbert expected the project to become local knowledge, but with a little care, the armed force would be in the Territory before a newspaper could pick up the story. Tolbert knew that Marshal Yoes would take precautions against the possibilities of a Territorial newspaper getting the story before the lawmen could surround the Christie fort.

Arriving in Fort Smith and joining John Tolbert's squad, the heavily armed group aroused no undue interest. Fort Smith was accustomed to armed men.

Boarding the train at the Fort Smith depot and joining the Clarksville contingent were Bill Ellis of Hartshorne, I.T., and E. B. Ratterree of Poteau, also in the Territory. John Tolbert introduced the seventeen-year-old posseman, Harry Clayland. Last to board was G. S. White, with his list of supplies.

As the swaying "peavine" picked up speed, Tolbert sought out White, who had charge of certain arrangements at West Fork, his home town.

"Cap," said Tolbert, "Marshal Yoes told me about three fellers up in Bentonville. He had promised them that if the opportunity came, they could serve as possemen. They are going to meet us at West Fork. One of them is Dan Maples' son. The other two are Jefferson and Peel."

"Sure," replied White, "I know them. I can understand their wanting to come along. I knew Dan Maples pretty well, and that town was sure ripped up about his getting murdered. Maples' boy, Sam, was just a young'un the last time I saw him, but he must be a grown man now. The three of them no doubt will make good possemen if Marshal Yoes says so. And, they are prominent people in Bentonville."

Tolbert nodded his agreement, and as an afterthought, White added:

"Now that I think of it, it was common talk in Bentonville about Sam Maples swearing an oath that if he ever got the chance, he was going after the man that killed his daddy.

White outlined to Tolbert the preparations he had made at West Fork. Three days before, after studying the October 11 attack on Christie's fort, both men agreed that rifles and pistols alone were not enough. White was of the opinion that, before very long, the U. S. Army would be sent in to flush Christie out. If that happened, White theorized, the army would use a field piece on the stout log fort. Why not procure a big gun? White had located a cannon at Coffeyville, Kansas, just across the border. Quick arrangements were made with the owner, a blacksmith who had built the gun, and with a supply of forty conical projectiles, the gun was shipped by rail to West Fork.

White leaned forward in his coach seat and tapped a large wooden box that was shoved underneath.

"Got enough explosives here to blow this train clear back to Fort Smith. There are thirty tins—one pound each—of black powder for the cannon, a half dozen sticks of heavy-duty dynamite, some fuses, and three big boxes of matches."

"Good," said Tolbert. "I checked the ammunition for the boys, we ought to have plenty."

The train labored through the pass in the Boston Mountain range, and before long, it hooted a signal for the West Fork station.

Deputy Marshal Gus York, who also lived at West Fork, was waiting with his neat little wagon and a pair of small, yellowish-brown mules that looked to have the endurance of percherons.

"Howdy, gents," he called, as the posse clambered off the train with their trappings of war, "here are three Benton-ville men who want to join up. Meet George Jefferson, Mack Peel, and Sam Maples."

Tolbert acknowledged the introductions. The two older men, Jefferson and Peel, were well armed and gave every appearance of being able to take care of themselves. Sam Maples was an affable enough young man, but Tolbert could detect the deep hatred that was burning inside the man.

"Can you use that Colt you got stuck in your belt?"

"Been practicing since I was sixteen," replied Maples.

"He has served as a posseman for Benton County officers," offered Peel. "The sheriff up there thinks that he would like to have Sam on his force."

Tolbert knew the sheriff, and he nodded his approval.

"Everybody in Bentonville has a grudge against your man, Christie," remarked Jefferson.

"All right," said Tolbert, "glad to have you men along. White will swear you in and give you the details. I have to see about getting our stuff loaded."

Sending Becky Polk into the little town for the necessary food supplies, Tolbert, with the help of York and the massive Ratterree, loaded the heavy box of explosives into the wagon.

York had already loaded the cannon. He pulled aside a heavy sheet of canvas. The thick barrel of the gun was four feet in length, and it had a one-inch bore. The barrel was solidly mounted on an oak carriage that was bound with strap iron. Although the barrel had a screw wheel for elevation, windage adjustment would have to be accomplished by means of a crowbar. There were no wheels on the gun carriage.

"Reckon that thing's big enough?" questioned York. "It's heavier'n hell, but the bore ain't so big."

"I don't know," answered Tolbert, his breath wheezing slightly from the exertion of loading the explosives.

"We brought the bullet-shaped slugs instead of the round balls for that reason. Maybe they will wedge in, when they hit, and split the walls of the fort."

"Your horses are at my place," said York, "Enos Mills and Jim Birkitt are saddling them up."

For Tolbert's information, York added:

"I had a young feller lined up to go as a posseman, Bill Robinson by name. But, when I went to get him, I found out that he had promised to get married today."

Tolbert laughed.

"I won't be able to go either," York continued. "I got a warrant for a feller up the other side of Fayetteville. You fellers are to use the wagon, though."

Tolbert was disappointed at the thought of not having the good-natured York along.

"Well, it's a good thing those three Bentonville fellers showed up."

"You got a good pair of deputies in Mills and Birkitt. They helped me load the cannon into the wagon. Why, if you put Birkitt with that fellow, Ratterree, that came up with you, you've got the equivalent of four men!"

Tolbert grinned. He knew Mills and Birkitt well. Mills, a blacksmith by profession from nearby Sulphur City, had been a federal lawman for many years. Birkitt stood six feet three inches in height, and while he was not in the same weight class as the ponderous Ratterree, he was a man of commanding size. The dark-complected Birkitt, who had seen service during the late war in the Illinois Infantry, had been sheriff of Washington County prior to his federal service. G. S. White had selected excellent additions to the posse.

Becky Polk returned with his groceries, and Tolbert helped him stash the packages in the wagon bed.

"Well," observed Becky, searching for a nook to place the last package, "there won't be any room in here for company."

With the loaded wagon following, Tolbert and his men struck out for York's home. York cast his eye at the sun.

"You fellers will just have time to reach the J. F. Summers store. It is due west of here, right on the border of the Cherokee Nation. He is expecting you, and will provide sleeping for the night. Cherokee Sheriff Ben Knight will be there by the time you pull in. You couldn't find a better guide for the country around Christie's place."

Tolbert nodded. Knight was a key man in his plans, for the posse would leave the route to Tahlequah when they approached the Christie place, and follow trails to a point on the east side of the fort. Selecting the correct trails would be a job for a man thoroughly familiar with the terrain.

The posse mounted the horses at York's place, shaking hands. York added:

"Charley Copeland and Heck Bruner will be at Summers' post, too. It is a closer place than here for them to join you, they are from Siloam Springs."

The band of lawmen made good time en route to the Summers' store, traveling via Hogeye and Cane Hill, over a narrow but firm road. The little mules, despite the heavy load they were pulling, frequently broke into a trot. True to York's prediction, the late fall sun was ready to dip into the vastness of the Indian Territory when they arrived at the crossroads settlement, which was named for the man who was to be their host. Charley Copeland and Heck Bruner came out of the big store building to greet them.

Tolbert shook hands with the seasoned deputy marshals. Copeland, a six-foot 170-pounder with an athletic build, had an unusually handsome face. The young deputy was as popular at pie supper socials and play-parties in the Territory as he was with fellow lawmen on manhunts. His large brown eyes sparkled with merriment as he greeted Tolbert. The grim nature of the posse's business did not dampen his jovial nature in the least. Of the same build but different temperament was Heck Bruner, a quiet man with rather fierce eyes. With a cheroot stub habitually clamped in his square jaws, he was just as formidable as he appeared. Bruner, at one time or another, had been on every major manhunt in the Territory in the past five years.

Ben Knight appeared on the porch of the store, accompanied by the proprietor.

Knight introduced himself. A full-blooded Cherokee, he moved with the sureness of a born athlete, and his well-worn six gun and rifle eloquently indicated his active profession.

Summers, a portly man, was greatly enthused at the prospect of a mighty effort brewing to put Christie out of commission.

"Raided my store twice," Summers boomed, shaking hands with Tolbert, "and I don't mind telling you I was plenty spooked both times. He is a tough-looking jasper since he got smashed in the face with a rifle ball."

Early the next morning, Summers was on hand to see the lawmen off. "About a mile west of here, on the same road, you'll come to the house where we had to board out two of your buddies—sorry I didn't have room for all of you."

Summers then distributed a can of sardines to each lawman, and he carefully placed two cans on the wagon seat beside Becky, for the two absent possemen.

"I poked a hole in the top of them and added a little pepper sauce. Compliments of the house. I hope you fellers catch that wild man."

The little mules were prancing in their eagerness for exercise, and the lawmen spurred their mounts into a trot. They soon picked up the two boarders, and as the morning sun splashed over the eastern horizon on that fall day of November 1, 1892, they pushed westward at a steady pace, crossing the boundary and entering the Cherokee Nation.

Tolbert did not set a fast pace. The posse had the full day in which to cover the distance to Christie's lair. Tolbert wanted to arrive during darkness.

As the group penetrated deeper into the Territory, Tolbert stood on his stirrups and cast a glance behind him. The posse, strung out along the narrow road, was much quieter, despite the cheerful Copeland's efforts to swap stories with the new men.

A brief respite from the monotonous jogging pace was gained when the group paused to pick up two more men near Baron Fork. Deputy Marshals Bill Smith and Tom Johnson were waiting beside the road. Johnson and Smith were of similar build, tall and rather slender, and each had a mustache almost as big as G. S. White's, but at that point the resemblance between the men ended.

Johnson was of Irish stock, fair-skinned with brown hair and mustache that had a faint trace of auburn. He was an affable man, but he was high-strung, and he became a grim adversary of Territorial hoodlums once he tackled a case. And he brooked no nonsense from his prisoner once a capture had been made.

Smith had the jet black hair and dark complexion that told of his Indian ancestry. His mother was a daughter of Chief Charley Journeycake, last Principal Chief of the Delawares, and his father was a white man who had served as a captain in the Union Cavalry during the war. With his dark eyes snapping underneath the brim of a black Stetson,

Smith was a dangerous-appearing man with his Colt and Winchester. He was an authority on Territorial law, referring constantly to a huge tome of Arkansas Reports that he owned. Smith was often called upon by his friends and neighbors to clear up a point of law, a service he willingly rendered.

The little mules pulled steadily all that day at the heavily loaded wagon, and when night came, they had finally lost their tendency to trot. Ben Knight moved to the head of the group, and he soon turned off the main road. In single file, the posse slowly threaded its way along dim trails. On steep inclines, the mules were rested for a spell after their labors on the grades.

Finally, a low whistle from Knight halted the posse. In the halting English common with many Cherokees of that day, he addressed Tolbert.

"Just over hill, Ned Christie fort. Move in closer when Dave Rusk come. He meet here. Leave horses tied here, but move wagon closer later. Keep quiet."

Tolbert indicated an order to dismount by swinging from his saddle. He loosened the saddle girth on his mount and slipped his Winchester from the saddle boot. Seeing the dim figure of Becky Polk in the gloom of the night, Tolbert called to him. Becky made his way around a couple of tethered horses, and joined by G. S. White, he approached Tolbert.

A fallen tree was nearby, and Tolbert settled himself on the trunk.

"Becky, when Dave Rusk gets here, we'll figure out a route to the fort for the wagon. Unload your cooking gear here, but be careful and don't bang any pans together."

As Becky turned away to do his chores, White untied the thong that secured his Fish Brand slicker to his saddle. He tossed the rolled garment to the ground and sat down on it. Others gathered, and soon the posse was comfortably seated in a semicircle. Tolbert placed his rifle across his knees.

"I've been noticing that rifle," observed White, "it looks like a Winchester, but it appears to be too light for an '86 model. That pistol grip on the stock is something new."

With a few deft motions, Tolbert took the rifle in half.

"It's a Winchester, all right. It's a take-down type, just like the '86 model, but it is a lighter gun. One of those rifle drummers was in Fort Smith the other day. He had a good line of Winchesters and he showed me this one; it is new, just out and not even in the Winchester catalogue yet. I figured that one of these days I might want to travel on a train and not let it be known that I was a lawman. I can pack this rifle in a valise, and keep my coat over my Colt, then no one would guess."

Tolbert handed the new model rifle to White, to pass around the group for inspection.

"Charley Copeland was on the October 11 raid," observed Tolbert, "now would be a good time to hear about it."

Copeland placed his cheroot under the heel of his boot and ground out the fire.

"It's cover you men got to think about, cover that will keep a bullet off. As you know by now, Christie will be inside a stout log fort. He has too many scouts around to be caught outside the fort. That fort is a two story affair and there are no windows in it. The top part has slits in the walls, Christie uses them to poke a rifle barrel through, and that is all you will have to aim at. All Christie needs is a glimpse of you and he'll put a bullet in your hide. It's a good thing we got a late fall, the leaves are still on the trees. As long as Christie can't see anybody, he won't shoot. When you do take a shot, make it a quick one and then duck, you won't know if Christie has spotted you or not."

"What about the spring," Tolbert asked.

"Christie can see the spring, down in the little valley

below the front of the fort. So, I don't advise any of you fellers getting thirsty."

"How many men do you suppose Christie has in that fort?" queried a voice in the darkness.

Tolbert answered the question:

"We don't have any idea, that is why we have tried to slip up on the fort. We aren't going to surprise Christie very much, but maybe he won't have time to corral much of his gang. The fewer shooters there are in the fort, the better off we'll be when we hit'er this morning."

"Dave Rusk can give us some pointers," Copeland remarked. "Hick Bruner and I are from the same town as Rusk, and we know for sure ole' Dave has been to that fort more times than anyone else."

"How come," remarked Oscar Blackard, turning to Bruner, "that some folks call you 'Hick,' and some call you 'Heck'?"

"Well," answered Bruner, "the family calls me 'Hick' from my name of Hickman, but so many people mixed it up with Heck Thomas that I just gave up trying to explain the difference."

"Same with me," said Tolbert. "I was christened 'Peden Edward,' from a family name, but when I started teaching school at Clarksville, I gave up trying to explain that it was 'Peden,' not 'Paden.'"

Copeland grinned. "Now, ah doan' see why folks would miss-unnerstan' the pro-nuncy-ashun of Pahden," he drawled, imitating Tolbert's Georgia brogue.

When the chuckles had died away, a voice piped up:

"Reckon we'll have to use that cannon?"

"Depend," drawled Tolbert, "if Christie won't give up, we may have to try her."

"What about the dynamite?" queried the same voice.

"Well," answered Tolbert, "it depends on the cannon. If we don't have any luck with the big gun, then we'll just have to figure a way to use the dynamite."

"It's too bad we haven't got a goose," observed Charley Copeland meditatively.

"Whut you want a goose for?" snorted Becky Polk. "We got plenty bacon, biscuit dough and beans."

"Well," answered Copeland, "I was just thinking of some way we might drop a bundle of dynamite down Christie's chimney."

The Johnson County men laughed, and with a grin, Tolbert raised his hand for silence. The mouth-drying tension that had been slowly mounting among the new men was suddenly broken. Tolbert had worked with enough "green" men to know that the most critical period was the lull that preceded the actual battle. He was pleased to see his Johnson County possemen pass the crucial time with ease.

Tolbert went over his battle plan again, emphasizing who was to form the cordon rings around the fort.

"You possemen," Tolbert explained, "will form the outer ring. You'll have two jobs. Watch in case anyone breaks out of the fort, and see to it that no one slips up on us from behind. We don't want any of Christie's men breaking through to join him, but I think we are too big an outfit for any of them to try it."

"We'll be all right, as long as Hick Bruner don't hear a hooty owl," remarked Charley Copeland.

Noticing Tolbert's baffled look, Copeland explained:

"After ol' Hick has pitched a camp—if he hears a hooty owl hooting, he'll break camp and move to a new spot."

Bruner chewed his cheroot stub in embarrassment.

"Well, hell," he growled, "ask Ben Knight if an owl hooting over a new camp ain't a sign that something bad is going to happen."

Knight nodded sagely. "Him right. Bad sign when owl warn you about sleeping."

"I think he's right," said Sam Maples. "My daddy was part Cherokee, and when he got a letter from the marshal to come over to Tahlequah, he had a warning. When my mother walked to the front gate with him, the day he left, a little bird swooped down and lit on his shoulder for an instant. My mother knew that this was an omen of death to the Cherokees, and she tried to talk him out of going. He just laughed, though, and when he got to Tahlequah, Christie killed him."

Becky Polk had a consultation with Tolbert. They decided, since the wind was blowing southward, away from Ned's fort, it would be safe to build a small shielded fire and brew some coffee. Soon, the soft, pungent aroma of Arbuckle's best grind filled the little clearing that contained the posse members and their horses. Becky broke out a huge box of salt crackers and dispensed them, and the group devoured the sardines that Summers had furnished. For a couple of hours the men discussed Cherokee superstitions and the battle plans.

A faint whistle from the nearby trail announced a visitor. Receiving an answering whistle, Dave Rusk strode into the clearing, leading his small saddle horse.

"Hell fire," announced the diminutive marshal, "that coffee smells powerful good."

Rusk was handed a tin cup, and he squatted down in the circle of men. After introductions were made to the new men in the group, Copeland remarked:

"Been telling the boys about that spring of Christie's. You got anything to add?"

Rusk promptly repeated Copeland's warning.

"It's plain suicide to go to it," he said. "We can drink out of the stream a little ways down from the spring—it's the same water."

"See anybody on your way in?" asked Tolbert.

"Nary a soul," answered Rusk, "but by daylight, I predict that a few curious folks will turn up."

Tolbert pulled his huge "turnip" watch from a pocket and thumbed open the cover. He surveyed the watch face with the help of a flickering match, and then he snapped the case shut.

"Almost four o'clock," he announced. "Let's go."

Paden Tolbert's deceptive, easygoing air vanished as he began the task of aligning his troops for battle.

"Dave, you will take the lead with the wagon."

Rusk nodded, and stepped over to the wagon. Loosening the reins from the brake handle, he went to the team and "got acquainted" with them. He rubbed the long ears of the gingery mules, and talked to them as though they were children.

"Becky," said Tolbert, "you stay here and red up the place, and then take your post. Knight, you can start out with the men, except Ratterree. I'll need him to help unload the cannon. Make your circles around the fort, and drop the men off as we planned."

Suddenly, the clarion notes of a lusty rooster broke the pre-dawn stillness.

"That Ned's rooster," stated Knight. Then, raising his hand as a signal, he stepped lithely away from the small camp fire. The designated men of the posse fell in behind him.

Accompanied by Tolbert, White, and the hulking Ratterree, Rusk led the team in a circuitous route south of the fort site until a small branch that was fed by Christie's spring gurgled softly around the hoofs of the mules. Pausing to permit the mules to drink the icy water, Rusk whispered:

"We'll go north now—right up the stream. It is not far, just before we get to the spring you will see a little clearing and an uprooted tree. This will be our cover, and we can aim this big gun right at Christie's front door. The fort is on top of the rise from this draw we are in, and if we have to use the gun, it will be uphill shooting."

"What about dogs?" queried Tolbert.

"He's got a pack of them," muttered Rusk, "and it is a wonder they haven't started yapping."

Carefully aiming a stream of tobacco juice away from the little stream, Rusk stooped over in order to see possible obstructions, and began a slow, threaded course upstream. By careful checking, he managed to keep the wheels of the wagon on the soft sand that formed the banks of the little creek. Occasionally, Tolbert and Ratterree would remove a rock to prevent the iron-shod wagon wheels clanking over it. Presently, Rusk straightened with a grunt, and paused.

"This is the spot," he announced.

The lawmen peered through the tangle of brush and tree trunks that covered the hillside. Against the faint gray color of the sky they could see the hulking outlines of a rectangular-shaped structure. Completing their survey, the four men maneuvered the wagon into position. With the aid of a crowbar, they slid the heavy gun carriage from the wagon bed. Using the iron bar again, they pried the gun until the muzzle pointed toward the fort. Wiping his face with a bandanna, Ratterree stalked away to take his post. Tolbert consulted his big watch.

"The others are in place by now," he announced hoarsely.

A faint crackling of twigs and whispered words across the cleared, wide path that led from the fort down to the spring indicated that the double cordon of men around the fort was completed. The vigil was not long. Dawn was preparing to break, and as the minutes ticked by, Tolbert could discern the outlines of a door in the fort.

"Only door there is," whispered Rusk, "unless Christie has dug a tunnel from the cellar to some place."

A creaking sound announced the opening of the fort door, and the watching lawmen stiffened. A figure emerged from the door, carrying a bucket. The man paused and stretched himself prodigiously. Several dogs that evidently had been sleeping near the log wall of the structure began barking discordantly.

"Take a bead on him, Dave," said Tolbert, "and I'll warn him."

Filling his lungs, Tolbert bellowed:

"Throw up your hands."

The startled man in front of the fort promptly forgot his errand to the spring. He dropped his bucket and sprang for the door. Instantly, Rusk's Winchester blasted the dawn air with a violent explosion.

As the echoes rumbled away through the hills, Rusk jerked the lever of his rifle and ejected the spent brass. Snapping the action shut with a fresh cartridge in the breech, he peered above the shelter of the prone tree trunk for a hasty check.

"The door is shut," he announced, seating himself on the ground. "Damn poor light for shooting, I don't know if I winged him or not."

Tolbert nodded slowly. He was methodically arranging opened boxes of cartridges on the ground. His project was on schedule, the timing was excellent and events had materialized just about as he had expected. Christie would not voluntarily leave his wooden stronghold. The Cherokee outlaw, along with an undetermined number of confederates, would have to be forced into the open.

Dave Rusk's next comment stated aloud Tolbert's thoughts.

"This is going to be one hell of a fight!"

12

CANNONADE IN GOING SNAKE DISTRICT

The rapid firing of twenty-four rifles and pistols heralded the daybreak of November 2, 1892, in the Going Snake District of the Cherokee Nation.

Precisely and to the second, the mighty barrage commenced, and for one full minute, a veritable hail of lead thudded and chunked into the double log walls of Ned Christie's rugged stronghold. The baying of the outlaw's pack of mongrels was drowned in the cascading thunder provided by the double ring of lawmen circumventing the fort. In unison, the barrage suddenly lifted. Outnumbered and intimidated by the iron throats that barked flame and lead, the dogs lent their quiet to the precipitant stillness.

Deputy Marshal Paden Tolbert leaned his hot Winchester against the huge log that formed his shelter.

"Now that he knows he is surrounded," the lawman announced, "I'll ask him to surrender."

Tolbert peered over the top of the log. The fort door, gleaming with the color of new wood, was quite plain now in the fresh light of the early morning. No sounds came from within the fort. Harry Clayland arrived for more courier duties, and Tolbert motioned to him to wait.

"Christie," called Tolbert, through cupped hands, "this is your chance to give up. You are surrounded by federal lawmen. We aim to stay here, and starve you out if we have to."

The minutes ticked by, and the lawmen eyed each other in the silence. Shrugging his shoulders, Tolbert called again:

"If there are any women in there, send them out—now!"

"Lay you a bet he sends the women out, and he stays," commented Rusk, aiming a stream of tobacco juice at a small stone.

The front door squealed, and the three lawmen instantly leveled their rifles. The door opened slightly and a hand appeared, waving a brightly colored blanket.

"Come out," shouted Tolbert.

An Indian woman came slowly out the door, followed by two more figures. They were women, and as they moved away from the door, one led a small boy.

Ben Knight, hearing the shouting, appeared in the clearing. Tolbert turned to him.

"Tell them to come down here, Ben."

Knight called in Cherokee, and the women walked toward the group.

"Keep heads down," warned Knight, softly.

Presently, the women and the boy were assembled in the clearing. Tolbert surveyed them for a moment.

"Ben, ask them who is in there with Christie."

To Knight's query the women shook their heads.

"Tell 'em to hit the trail for Bitting Springs," snapped Tolbert, "and not to come back."

The women eyed Tolbert uneasily as Knight converted the message to Cherokee. The marshal's normally pleasant face contained a pair of blue eyes as cold appearing as the icy little stream that flowed nearby. The woman holding the hand of the boy jerked her charge around and moved hastily away. The other two followed her.

"Follow 'em a ways," Tolbert said to Clayland.

Clayland shouldered his shotgun and swung off down the sandy bank of the little creek. Coming out of the thick underbrush, he could see the figures of the women as they reached the trail. Glancing back, they saw Clayland, and they quickly walked down the trail toward Bitting Springs. Quite a number of Cherokees had gathered at the point where the trail forded the creek. They were unarmed, eying Clayland impassively.

Clayland retraced his steps to the cannon site. Tolbert was speaking to Knight.

"Ben, I want to be sure Christie understands that we are not pulling out this time. Just tell him that he is in for a helluva fight."

Knight translated Tolbert's final message in a loud voice, but silence followed his words.

Clayland informed Tolbert of the visitors down at the ford. Tolbert nodded.

"Make the circle and tell the men to start firing at the slits when they hear us commence over here."

As Clayland left, Tolbert motioned to Knight.

"There are a bunch of people down at the ford. Go down there and see if Ned's daddy is there. If he is, tell him that he is welcome to come up and try to talk to Ned, but that we are not calling off the fight this time."

Knight shook his head in doubt, but he walked away downstream.

Tolbert called across the cleared lane on his left.

"John?"

"Here," replied John Tolbert, invisible behind his tree-trunk concealment. "Heck Bruner and Charley Copeland are right beside me."

"You three open up on the slits when Rusk starts firing," Tolbert directed, "and we will give Ned something to think about. I am going around to the south and check on Bowman."

Tolbert made his way to Bowman's place of shelter. Nearby was the huge form of Ratterree.

"Wess," Tolbert greeted his friend, "we are in for a fight."

Bowman nodded. "I know, Clayland just passed by."

"Young Sam Maples is just behind you," Tolbert said, dropping his voice to a whisper. "Keep an eye on him. He may take a notion to charge that fort."

Tolbert glanced at his watch. "Time about up. Good luck."

As Tolbert returned to the cannon site, Dave Rusk poked his rifle barrel over the top of the log and squeezed off a shot. He ducked immediately, but his reflexes were not quite speedy enough. A shot blasted from the fort, and as he fell prone behind the log, Rusk felt a familiar, angry tug on the crown of his hat. Rolling over, he pulled the headpiece off and ruefully surveyed the rude bullet tear.

Ben Knight returned to the cannon site, but before he could report to Tolbert, a young Cherokee girl suddenly materialized from the brush on the opposite side of the little stream. She easily leaped across.

"Baby in fort," she announced.

Knight eyed her for a moment.

"Women would never leave baby in fort," he told Tolbert.

Turning to the woman, Knight suddenly snatched a large apron she was wearing, snapping the drawstring in the process. Holding up the garment, he reached into its folds and extracted five boxes of .44-caliber cartridges.

"Well, shut my mouth," exclaimed the surprised Tolbert.

Knight growled a few Cherokee words, and the woman scuttled away into the brush.

"Told her we might send her down to see Judge Parker," Knight remarked, the faint flicker of a smile on his dark features.

"Did you find Christie's daddy down there?" asked Tolbert.

Knight nodded. He raised his voice in order to be heard over the racket of gunfire as the Christie battle settled down to a grim game of deadly pot-shots.

"He say—no use to talk."

For hours the battle continued, and the day developed

into a windy fall afternoon. Harry Clayland appeared at the cannon site with his periodic reports.

"What's the news?" Tolbert asked, tilting his Stetson to the back of his head.

"By gosh," Clayland replied, his eyes big, "every man has a bullet hole or two through his clothes, but nary a one of them is even scratched."

G. S. White whistled softly. "Just a matter of time. The Good Lord has been on our side so far."

Tolbert nodded, and as though to cap his thoughts, Dave Rusk tore his hat from his head and flung it on the ground. It was the third bullet to strike the hat, and now the crown was almost completely gone.

"This business of popping up and jerking a shot, and popping back is not going to cut it," snapped Rusk, savagely kicking his ruined hat.

"Paden," called John Tolbert from across the lane. "Tom Johnson has an idea. He is circling around to come over and show you."

Tolbert raised his voice in order to be heard above the incessant rifle fire:

"We just might try it." Then he added, "You and Heck doing all right?"

"Got a bullet through my hat brim," came John's answer. "Heck is all right. Charley has gone to get some water for us."

"I know," replied Tolbert. "He just left here with a bucketful."

Tom Johnson appeared with a long rifle under his arm. The other arm was burdened with a bundle of newly cut slender sticks, some rags and a can of coal oil from Becky's supplies.

"This is my spare gun," Johnson said with a grin, noticing Tolbert's quizzical look. "We may be able to use an Indian trick on Ned."

Tolbert caught on immediately. He hefted Johnson's .45-70-caliber single-shot Springfield rifle.

"Flaming arrows," he said, with a smile.

Johnson quickly tied a small bundle of rags tightly on one end of a stick. He poured a generous quantity of coal oil on the rags and then set a match to it. A satisfactory flame immediately engulfed the knobby end of the stick. Thrusting the bare end of the stick down the muzzle of the rifle, he lifted it to his shoulder and fired in the direction of the fort.

The flaming stick arched across the clearing and struck the front wall of the fort with an audible thud, but it bounced away and fell to the ground, burning harmlessly.

"Try another," urged White.

Johnson was already busy making up another "arrow." This time, the stick struck the wall in a true line and remained imbedded in a log, quivering violently. Cheers of the lawmen gathered in the front of the fort quickly died away, however. It was obvious that the heavy log would not ignite from such a feeble fire.

"Green wood," snorted Rusk.

He was right. Earlier in the day Clayland had reported coming across a steam boiler and engine mounted on wheels. The rig was hooked up to a sawmill that Christie had used to cut his building materials. The structure and its materials were only a few months old.

Christie had spotted the flaming arrows. He spitefully sent a number of quick shots in the direction of the cannon site, but no one was visible to him and his bullets zipped angrily but impotently through the foliage.

"Well," said Tolbert, brushing away a bullet-severed brown leaf that had settled on his shoulder, "see if you can stab one into the roof."

Johnson took careful aim, but the stick proved erratic. Smoking like a skyrocket, the arrow sailed high above the roof of the fort and vanished from view. A distant whoop came from the far side of the fort.

"You woke up one of your men that time, Paden," re-marked Copeland, from across the lane.

Johnson made up another arrow. With the boom of the heavy rifle, the stick sailed straight for the roof, snapping in two when it struck. The heavier end, though, was embedded securely under one of the thick shakes.

The lawmen watched anxiously for several minutes, ignoring Christie's angry rifle fire. The rags burned brightly enough, but eventually they smoldered, and a puff of dark smoke announced the failure of the experiment. The shake roof was as green as the rest of the building.

Tolbert eyed the cannon.

"I was thinking the same thing," said White, pulling at his long mustache.

Tolbert obtained a number of projectiles from the wagon, and White selected a tin of powder. Using one of Becky's tin cups, White poured the measure of shiny, granular black powder down the cannon muzzle. Using an ash pole provided for the purpose, Tolbert inserted one of the projectiles and shoved it down the muzzle as far as it would go. White carefully poured a small amount of powder down the touch hole at the thick breech of the gun.

Clayland appeared on schedule, and Tolbert gave him new orders.

"Tell the men on the east side to stay behind big tree trunks; we are going to try the cannon."

Clayland left at a trot, and White knelt behind the gun and sighted along the barrel. Using the crowbar, Tolbert pried the gun carriage until White was satisfied that the muzzle was aimed directly at the front wall of the fort.

Tolbert leaned against the gun barrel and mopped his face with a bandanna, his labored breathing rasping in his throat. Presently, a distant shout announced that the lawmen on the opposite side of the fort had taken precautionary cover.

Tolbert picked up one of Johnson's prepared arrows. With the long stick, he could apply flame to the touch hole of the cannon, and be clear of the recoil of the piece as it discharged. Striking a match on the seat of his trousers, Tolbert ignited the oil-soaked knob of cloth on the end of the stick, and carefully applied the flame to the touch hole.

Instantly, the muzzle of the cannon belched a spurt of orange flame. As the gun carriage bounced with recoil, a great, billowing cloud of acrid blue gun smoke enveloped the figures around the gun. Almost in unison with the bellow of the heavy report, the gunners heard the cast-iron projectile strike the wall of the fort.

The smoke rolled away quickly on the spanking breeze, and peering anxiously, the lawmen could see a raw gash in a log some six feet above the door jamb. Though cutting a sizable gouge of wood, the iron slug had not harmed the ponderous wall.

Ned Christie, no doubt startled at the loud report and powerful jar against the wall, did not panic. The embittered outlaw cinched the final outcome of the battle for the disappointed lawmen. As the heavy echoes of the cannon shot subsided, they could hear the weird gobbling sound that was the death cry of the Cherokee.

Stubbornly prying the gun into place, Tolbert wiped his perspiring face.

"May as well lob a few at him," he said, his features reflecting his disappointment.

"Dammit," said Rusk, "what we need is a twelve-pounder 'Napoleon'; she'd chop those walls down."

For an hour the weary men loaded the gun and fired and then laboriously repositioned it after each shot. Other than gouging and slashing the walls, the slugs had little effect. A few embedded jarringly into the logs, but most of the slugs rebounded sharply and fell helter-skelter around the clearing. Even an assault on the roof brought little result. The slugs tore harmlessly through the shakes, dislodging a few in the process. The roof maneuver brought howls of protest from the secreted lawmen on the east side of the fort. The one pound slugs sounded much larger than their actual size as they thudded into tree trunks, or sliced off limbs that fell with a crash.

Tolbert gagged and coughed as a cloud of gun smoke spurted from the cannon muzzle and billowed around his head.

"I hear tell," remarked White, spitting vigorously on the ground in an effort to remove the acrid taste, "that a new gunpowder will be on the market soon, a smokeless type, and a lot more powerful than black powder."

"Well," gasped Tolbert, wiping his streaming eyes, "it's too damn bad we haven't got a jug of it now. I guess we may as well give up on this gun."

"Try one more shot, and use about a half cup more powder," urged Clayland.

With nothing to lose, White poured the extra quantity of gunpowder down the muzzle. Applying his lighted stick, Tolbert set off the charge, and the lawmen knew instantly that the cannon was done for. With a muffled report, the breech split at the touch hole, and the projectile skipped across the clearing, digging up divots of brown grass.

"What the hell happened?" called Copeland, unable to see the cannon site from his post across the lane.

"Cannon busted," answered Tolbert, surveying the ruined cannon. In a moment, his shoulders straightened, and he turned to Clayland.

"Pass the word. Becky has gone down to the camp site, and he has grub ready by now. Start the men, two at a time as planned, and we'll get everybody fed. At sundown, we'll have a council of war."

"Even if it didn't work," observed Copeland, "I'll bet this is the first time a cannon was used trying to bring an outlaw in."

Tolbert walked to the little stream. Sprawling on his stomach, he took a long drink of the cold water, and then washed the black gun-smoke stains from his face. Turning to White he said:

"Did you notice those old wagon wheels at the edge of the clearing, toward us?"

White nodded. "The wheels are on a rear axle, all that's left of Ned's wagon. Copeland was in the bunch when they used the wagon trying to set the fort on fire."

"Charley was the one who slung some dynamite, too," said Rusk. "Fuse came out though, and it didn't go off."

Tolbert rubbed his chin that was dark and sandpapery with the beginnings of a beard.

"We'll get Charley in on this."

Rusk and White nodded. Copeland, though still in his twenties, had a lengthy law enforcement career. He had been city marshal of Siloam Springs, Arkansas, prior to his federal service. The good-natured fellow had not only the nerve but the athletic prowess for the feat Tolbert had in mind.

"When it gets dark, we'll drag those wheels back into the woods where we can work on them," Tolbert said, picking up one of Johnson's sticks. With the stick, he traced out his idea on the sandy bank of the little creek. White and Rusk agreed that it was a practical way to get a charge of dynamite against a wall of the fort, and give the lawmen a chance to stay alive.

When darkness came, the lawmen succeeded in rolling the wheels deep into the woods so that a lantern could be safely used. With heavy planking found at the site of Ned's sawmill, they fashioned a crude but effective wooden shield. Copeland procured the tongue of the wagon and attached it to the axle. Rusk, catching the idea, improved on the installation.

"I'll brace her with a couple of two by heavies," he said, selecting a couple of suitable pieces from the pile of scrap lumber brought from the sawmill. The heavy shield was then attached to the axle of the wheels, and Copeland picked up the tongue and moved it from side to side.

"We can steer this thing," he remarked, "it looks like an overgrown lawn mower."

Tolbert removed the wheels from the axle that had squalled loudly when removed from the clearing. He liberally greased the axles with globs of lard obtained from Becky's chuck supplies, and replaced the wheels.

It was after midnight, November 3, when the mobile breastwork finally met the approval of the lawmen. Deputy Marshal Bill Smith joined the group. Tolbert knew of Smith's uncanny ability to fire a rifle rapidly with great accuracy. For the same reason, Tolbert sent for posseman Bill Ellis, who was captain of the Coal and Iron Police, a company organization in the mining center of Hartshorne. Rusk would take up his old post at the cannon site and lay down the principal cover barrage. Charley Copeland would handle the dynamite.

"Just call us 'the dynamiters' after this," commented Copeland, busily wiring six sticks of dynamite together. "If we could dig a hole under the wall, this is a heavy enough charge to wreck the fort."

Tolbert shook his head. He knew that if given half a chance, Copeland would attempt such a feat.

"Nope," he said, "we have gotten this far without anyone getting killed. Let's keep it that way."

Tolbert, however, was under no illusions concerning the danger of the plan they were preparing to execute. The cordons had been informed when to lay down their diversionary barrage, but the fact still remained, the five lawmen making the run to the wall of the fort would have only their makeshift barricade on wheels to protect them from instant death. They carefully checked their Winchesters for smooth lever operation and full magazines.

Charley Copeland found a handy small stub of a limb on a tree trunk. He carefully hung his Winchester and his Stetson on the projection and unholstered his Colt. One of his hands would be occupied with dynamite and in case of need for a firearm, his revolver would be the better weapon.

The Colt single-action Army Model six-shooter was normally carried with only five of the chambers loaded, permitting the big hammer to rest on the empty sixth chamber. The big revolver had no safety feature otherwise. Copeland eared back the hammer of his weapon to the half-cock notch and flipped open the loading gate. Rotating the cylinder until the conventional empty chamber was exposed, he slipped in a cartridge, and then gently eased the hammer down. Reholstering the Colt, Copeland observed:

"A full house is hard to beat."

Tolbert leaned close to the yellow light of the lantern and extracted his big watch. The others rose to their feet, and Tolbert snapped the cover of his watch.

"Let's go," he said.

Reaching out, Tolbert pressed the lever that raised the glass of the lantern. Taking a deep breath, he blew out the flame. As if the extinguishing of the lantern had been a signal, the cordon set up its barrage.

The lawmen quickly maneuvered the wheels through the forest to the clearing surrounding the fort. Without pausing they trotted with the ungainly contraption, and had gained perhaps three quarters of the distance to the fort before Christie, or one of the two confederates who the lawmen had long since determined were holed up with the outlaw, spied the moving dark object headed toward the fort. The men behind the barricade tensed as bullets began whacking viciously into the heavy planking. One slug struck the iron tire of one of the wheels, and ricocheted into the darkness— howling banefully.

"Now," yelled Tolbert.

The crouching Copeland, with steady hand, struck a match and held it to the fuse of the deadly bundle in his fist. As soon as the fuse began sputtering with a life of its own, Tolbert and White dropped the tongue and stepped to the right of the shield, dropping to kneeling positions. Their Winchesters became things alive as they rapidly worked the levers—pumping shot after shot into the wall of the fort where they estimated the slits to be. Simultaneously, Ellis and Smith knelt on the opposite side of the breastwork, and began masterful jobs of fast shooting.

The only real targets the lawmen had were the winking orange spots of gunfire from the slits in the wall before them.

Charley Copeland leaped from behind the breastwork and raced like a cheetah for the wall, sparks from the burning fuse trailing fitfully behind him. Reaching the wall, he laid the bundle snugly against the base. With scarcely a pause, he wheeled and sped for the breastwork.

The barrage at the breastwork proved effective, no outlaw bullets found Copeland as he dived behind the shelter. Immediately, Copeland grasped the tongue of the rig, and the riflemen jumped to safety. The crouching lawmen began as fast a retreat as they could manage. Christie, knowing that something unusual was afoot, made his unearthly gobbling sound and began a rifle fire that was as fast as the lawmen's staccato Winchester talk. They could feel the jarring impacts of Christie's bullets through their handholds on the rig.

The lawmen almost reached the forest when the explosion came. It was a fearful blast that lit up the sky, and many folks later claimed they heard the boom in distant Tahlequah. The fleeing dynamiters felt the powerful concussion on the breastwork as they reached the forest.

All gunfire had ceased abruptly, and the breathless lawmen peered at the fort from the shelter of tree trunks. Debris flung high into the air by the mighty explosion was thudding to the ground. For a while, they could discern little through the haze of dust and foggy smoke, but day was breaking fast. Presently, a flickering light could be seen. The light grew steadily stronger until the officers could see a huge, gaping hole in the south wall of the fort. The stronghold was burning from the inside.

Still panting from his exertions, White strained his eyes in the murky dawn. As the fire mounted, the fruits of the lawmen's efforts was revealed. The son of a minister, White was a rather devout man.

"The Good Lord was with us that time," he remarked gravely.

"Ol' Ned's cook stove has the inside wood dried out," observed Copeland, as the flames mounted higher, and the crackling and popping of burning wood could be heard distinctly.

"You must be right, Charley," said Tolbert, leveling his rifle across a convenient tree limb. "That fire has got hold of something besides green wood."

The other lawmen leveled their rifles, waiting for Christie's next move—if he hadn't been knocked out or killed by the explosion. Thick smoke began billowing from the ruined fort as the fire tackled the green wood. The heavy smoke was wafted southward by the ever-present wind in a ground-hugging pall.

Suddenly, two rifle shots sounded loudly. The shots were some distance from the fort.

"I'd better take a look," said Tolbert, motioning for the others to remain on guard.

As Tolbert began working his way in the direction of the shots, he thought fleetingly that perhaps some of Ned's friends had belatedly come to his aid. Tolbert immediately dismissed the thought, for his cordon had maintained a sharp vigil for just such an event. The only visitors sighted were the onlookers down at the ford, and they were not there to aid Christie.

Tolbert was reminded of the Sydney Wallace case in Johnson County. At first, Sid had the backing of the community, but as he became a lawless figure, folks had shied away from him.

Tolbert halted in his tracks as the unmistakable boom of a large-caliber revolver in rapid discharge shook the morning air. Tolbert broke into a run. The shots were nearby, at the location Wess Bowman had chosen for the siege of Ned's fort.

Coming abruptly to the place of Bowman's concealment, Tolbert breathed a sigh of relief as he saw the young deputy marshal's slender figure standing beside the giant Ratterree. They were gazing down at the sprawled figure of an extremely tall Indian.

"Christie!"

Bowman nodded calmly. Sam Maples was standing nearby, reloading his big Colt. Maples eyed Tolbert rather defiantly.

"I didn't kill him, but he sure as hell is toting some lead in his gizzard."

"What happened?" Tolbert was a little puzzled.

"Criminy," breathed Ratterree. "I thought Christie had Bowman for sure. He just popped out of that smoke, running like hell. He nearly run over Bowman before they saw each other."

"Christie must have come out of that hole in the wall," Bowman explained. "Anyhow, he followed the hanging smoke and he was right on top of me when I saw him. He looked as surprised as I was, and he jerked off a shot from his rifle right in my face."

"Well, he was running so fast that he was by me before I could get off a shot. I wheeled and fired my rifle from the hip. The bullet hit him behind his ear, and I believe he was dead before he hit the ground."

"And then, Maples ran up and emptied his six-shooter into him."

"Right," said Maples, holstering his revolver, "I have been waiting five years to drill that killer."

Bowman gingerly felt of his cheek. Tolbert peered closely. "You got a powder burn."

Ratterree chimed in. "That's about as close as you can get a rifle fired at your face—and not feel some lead."

The cordon of lawmen closed in on the ruined fort, rifles ready in case more outlaws emerged. The fight, however, was over.

Ben Knight was startled to hear moans of anguish coming from the lower floor of the building. Tolbert, Rusk and Knight dashed inside and hauled a terrified young Cherokee from the cellar. The lad's face on one side and one of his forearms were disfigured by huge, watery blisters.

"It's Charley Soldier-Hair," exclaimed Knight, and he assured the youth in Cherokee that he would not be harmed. G. S. White procured some lard from Becky's dwindling supplies and smeared the young Cherokee's burns.

"Take him to Tahlequah and get a doctor," Tolbert ordered Knight.

Noticing several boxes on the ground floor of the blazing building, Tolbert and Rusk took a chance and went back. The burning floor above them was threatening to collapse, and the two lawmen each grabbed a box and bolted for the door. The diminutive Rusk collided with the door that was hanging askew from the force of the dynamite explosion. The door tore loose, and the marshal and his box spilled to the ground. Rusk picked himself up and examined the contents. It proved to be several bolts of velvet cloth.

Tolbert set his box down a safe distance from the burning fort, and the first floor fell with a crash.

"If there is anyone left in there," Tolbert observed, "he is a roasted possum now."

Tolbert was thinking of the third person they knew had been with Christie. Later, they discovered that it was Arch Wolf, and he had evidently made his escape at the time Christie had bolted out.

Curious, Rusk removed the lid of the box Tolbert had rescued. It contained a number of new Stetson hats.

"Well, now," chortled Rusk, "here's where I replace my hat."

He removed his bullet-torn hat and tossed it to the ground.

He tried on a couple of the new hats, and then he noticed the dealer's name that was stamped in gilt letters on the leather sweat bands of the new head pieces.

D. V. RUSK, GEN'L MERCHANDISE, OAKS, I.T.

"Hell fire," exploded Rusk, "this is some of the loot from my store!"

The chilly morning wore on, and Ned Christie's fort was reduced to burned rubble. Tolbert ordered the growing crowd of spectators to keep back. He was astonished that there was even a photographer in the little throng.

"I have a suggestion," remarked White, as the lawmen prepared to depart. "We should take Christie's body to Fayetteville and get a doctor's certificate of death. We can catch a train for Fort Smith there."

White's idea made sense, as the older lawmen in the group well knew. When a felon with a large reward on his head was killed in the process of justice, an official document attesting the cause of death was a material aid in winding up the case.

Rusk picked up the fort door he knocked loose.

"This is just what we need."

Rusk carried the door to where Christie's body lay. He rolled the corpse onto the stout wooden surface. Arranging the long legs, he bound them together with a bit of rope, and placing the hands on the chest, he secured the arms. Copeland grasped one end of the door, and Ratterree took the other end in his big hands. The two men carried the corpse down to the cannon site.

Becky had already broken camp, and his tin ware and the remains of his food supply were stored in the wagon bed. Arranging the equipment in the forward end of the bed, the lawmen placed the tightly roped corpse aboard. Becky unfolded the canvas and covered the body.

They reached Summers' store by nightfall, and again, the

lawmen were overnight guests of the jubilant Summers, who considered the death of Christie to be a milestone in the course of events for that section of the country.

The next day the posse made the trip to Fayetteville, putting up the mules at a livery stable on the southwest corner of the court square. Tolbert politely but firmly refused to uncover Christie's body for the sake of the growing crowd of curious onlookers. Dr. H. D. Wood was summoned to issue the death certificate. With train time nearing, the posse hired a hack to transport Christie's body to the railroad station. The crowd there was even larger.

Christie's body was placed on a high-wheel baggage cart, and Bowman attempted to lose himself, but Copeland was too quick for him.

"Fellows," he boomed to the crowd of students, "since you are skipping school to see the man that got Ned Christie, here he is, Deputy Marshal Wess Bowman."

A wave of applause came, and the embarrassed Bowman had to explain the powder burn on his cheek, which would heal and leave a tattoo of black specks.

"Any of you fellows get shot?"

"Nope," replied Bowman, "we were lucky."

"How many shots did you fire?"

"Well, that would be hard to say, at least for the rifles and pistols. We shot off the cannon about thirty times, and our cook-posseman, who kinda has a habit of keeping track of supplies, subtracted the ammunition we have left from what we started out with. He figures we fired two thousand shots."

Several exclamations came from the crowd. One eager voice asked:

"Who fired the most shots?"

Bowman shrugged. "What does it matter? Everyone who fired a shot was exposed for a second to Christie."

The hoot of the approaching Fort Smith train permitted Bowman to break away, and the posse boarded the train.

Arriving in Fort Smith, the lawmen transported Christie's body to the Federal building, to be met by a huge and jovial Marshal Yoes and all the deputy marshals who happened to be in Fort Smith that day. As questions and answers were exchanged, a civic group approached Marshal Yoes. They wanted the body of Christie put on display for the school children of Fort Smith.

G. S. White voiced his opinion. "It just might be a good idea. There is nothing sadder than a boy who has gotten himself mixed up in crime."

Tolbert guessed that White was thinking of Charlie Soldier-Hair.

"Well," agreed the Marshal, "we'll leave it here on the porch for the afternoon. Ben Knight called from Tahlequah and says that Christie's family will claim the body. They'll be here some time tonight."

A photographer in the crowd requested a picture. Deputy Marshal Hugh Harp, before the man could snap his picture, stuck a Winchester in Christie's stiffened arms.

"This feller died by the gun, he ought to have his picture made with one."

More requests came for photographs, and the lawmen reported to Gannaway's Studio for pictures. It was some time before Tolbert was free to seek a hotel room. Copeland was also seeking obscurity and rest for the remainder of the day. A group of admiring people had taken up a collection and purchased a fine, engraved Winchester, and had presented it to Copeland.

Examining the beautiful weapon, Tolbert remarked:

"You better hide, before Bowman sees this. He'll kid the pants off you."

In the quiet of his hotel room, Tolbert pulled the scarred boots with some difficulty from his aching feet. He stretched out with a sigh on the big bed that occupied most of the little room. Drowsily, he reflected on the events of the past three days.

Tolbert placed his muscular arms under his head and thought of the day Wess Bowman had received his commission as deputy marshal. Judge Parker had greeted the serious-faced young fellow.

"This is a dangerous job," the judge had said, "and you are a brave man, or you would not be standing here before me. But you will need more than courage to handle the job you have sworn to do. You'll need a good Winchester rifle and a good horse."

Tolbert recalled the confusion and excitement on the big porch of the Federal building, when they had carried Ned Christie's body up the steps and leaned it against the wall. The climax of the whole series of events the past few days, for Tolbert, was the appearance of white-haired Judge Parker on the porch to offer his congratulations. The judge had eyed the corpse of Christie, and then turned to Bowman.

"I see," the big jurist had said, his piercing eyes twinkling, "that you had a good Winchester!"

13

THE COOK GANG

"Yes, sir, right on the street in Catoosa, this feller whips out a big sheath knife, and cuts the other feller's head clean off!"

Walter "Spunky" Taylor was describing a fight scene to Deputy Marshal Paden Tolbert. Taylor had been sworn into federal service June 27, 1893, and George Crump, replacing Jacob Yoes as Chief Marshal, requested Tolbert to work with Taylor because of his previous acquaintance with the new man.

Tolbert welcomed the assignment to train Taylor, for he would then be selecting only the whiskey warrants for a couple of months. Tolbert's assignments, since the Christie battle in the fall of the year before, had all been deep in the Territory. It would be good to work near Fort Smith for a while.

"So, you have been serving as city marshal of Catoosa since you left Arkansas," observed Tolbert.

Spunky Taylor nodded. "Yes, and that job actually led me into asking for federal service."

"They gave you a tough town to police," observed Tolbert. "Because of its location most of the big cattle ranches in the Cherokee Nation clear through there, to ship their cattle. Being close to the Verdigris Bottoms makes it handy for a feller on the scout that is hiding out in those thickets.

They can slip into town when the herds are brought in, and no one will notice."

"Actually," said Taylor, "those hard-cases from the Bottoms never did cause me any real trouble. After all, they were dodging the law. It's the damn senseless hell-raising that got under my skin.

"Take those two fellers I was telling you about: You know how merchants will hang out a few ears of corn when they buy up a crop, so folks will know there is corn for sale? Well, there was a drunk 'shelling corn'—that's what they called it when they would decide to put some life into the town. They'll ride up and down the street, shooting with six guns at those clusters of corn hanging in front of a store. Naturally, everyone on the streets would duck inside somewhere. With those drunks hollering, and galloping their horses and shooting .45s, I can tell you it gets pretty noisy. When a bullet hits a cluster of corn, the ear will explode like popcorn going off.

"Well, this stranger comes into town right when a 'shelling' was taking place. He got off his horse right in front of a store that had a juicy bunch of corn hanging out. This one drunk didn't like it because the stranger was in the way, so he just up and shot him.

"The stranger was hit, but he managed to pull his iron and plug the drunk, knocking him out of his saddle. The man gets up, though, and charges the stranger, and they began to wrestle—with each other's bullet in their hides. It was a bloody mess, and the drunk got the other feller pushed back across a hitching rail. He jerks out a big sheath knife and cuts the stranger's throat grinning-wide. He didn't stop there, he just kept hacking until he had that feller's head cut clean off. Then he staggered over to a hitch post that had a pointed top. He was carrying that head by its hair, and he jammed it down on top of that sharp post. I'll admit, someone drilled that drunk with a rifle, and put him out for good. But, it was the sort of thing that made me quit. All I could do was to bang a drunk on his head and lock him up. I had little other authority."

Tolbert shook his head.

"Well, I don't have to tell you, now that you are a deputy marshal, that the jaspers we will be doing business with are a lot worse than those corn shellers at Catoosa."

Taylor was silent a few moments, contemplating the aspects of his new job.

"Well," he said at last, philosophically, "I reckon somebody has to police the Indian Territory."

In the weeks that followed, Tolbert requested a large number of whiskey warrants in order to acquaint Spunky Taylor with the Territory. Taylor's training period was relatively brief, and his progression to felony cases of more serious mien coincided with the advent of the newest "Terror" to strike the Indian Nations. The Bill Cook Gang appeared on the scene.

Bill Cook was an orphan boy of Cherokee lineage who had learned to rope, ride and shoot on various ranches in the Nations. Cook worked hard for his wages, and he was careful not to indulge in the wild spending sprees that most of his cowpoke companions looked forward to on paydays. However, the young puncher's industrious nature, and money were concentrated on an illegal project. He was buying whiskey and selling it to Indians at a profit.

Eventually, the federal law had a warrant for Bill Cook. He fled to New Mexico, sojourning there until he figured that it was safe to return. Upon arriving in Territory, he found that the law at Fort Smith had a long memory. He was apprehended and brought before Judge Parker. Usually, the big judge had little patience with young hoodlums, but Cook received a mild sentence of only forty days in the Fort Smith jail.

Judge Parker's leniency, however, was wasted. Once out

of jail Bill Cook, with his brother Jim, began a series of horse thefts to make money. The brothers became so efficient that Cherokee Bill, the scourge of the Territory, sought them out.

Crawford Goldsby, alias "Cherokee Bill," had parents of mixed blood, consisting of Mexican, Sioux, Cherokee and Negro, which did not indict Cherokee Bill of any crime, but a broken home had left its mark on him.

Much of Cherokee Bill's early life is shrouded in legends. It is recorded that at the age of twelve he killed a relative in an argument over some hogs. By the time he was eighteen years of age he was a husky fellow with a wild, unpredictable nature, and he had three killings charged against him. He was on the scout after shooting a man at a dance, and he figured that he needed companionship. He sought the Cook brothers, who were industriously operating around the Wagoner-Muskogee area.

During the months that Cherokee Bill was "preparing" himself for his bloody destiny, another series of events were formulating that were to have an even greater impact on the Territory. The Dawes Indian Commission was shaping up. The commission would change the destiny of the Indian just as surely, but without the gunsmoke violence, as the deeds of the federal lawmen were changing the society of the Indian Territory.

Veteran member of Congress Henry L. Dawes, from the State of Massachusetts, was an expert on Indian affairs. He had long championed government relations with Indian tribes on a fair basis. With the struggles between law and order factions and gangs of lawless men reaching a crescendo, even casual observers could see that the Indian Territory was indeed "out of pocket" in time. It was the last rugged frontier on the American scene where men still carried Colts and Winchesters because of a deadly necessity. The plight of the Indian, on whose soil the bloody battles were staged, was at all times a primary concern of Henry Dawes.

Wherever and whenever plans for future progress were made, or dreamed about, in the Territory, the factor of statehood was large. There were movements on every side that sponsored preparations for statehood petitioning.

On March 3, 1893, an act of Congress created the Dawes Indian Commission and Henry Dawes was appointed Chairman of the new group by President Grover Cleveland. Appointed as commissioners were Meredith Kidd of Indiana and Archibald S. McKennon of Arkansas.

Captain A. S. McKennon, a Confederate veteran, was a pioneer lawyer of Clarksville who served Johnson County as prosecuting attorney during the days when Paden Tolbert was a fledgling posseman and deputy sheriff.

The first meeting of the Dawes Commission was held in Washington in December 1893. The commission was charged with the task of negotiating with the Five Civilized Tribes for surrender of tribal lands. The commission was authorized to grant in exchange allotments of land in severalty. The process would be the first step in preparing the Indian for United States citizenship, which would abolish his tribal status. It was a necessary prelude to Oklahoma statehood.

With saddlebags instead of booted Winchesters, the Dawes Commission began its unprecedented task, riding the Chickasaw, Seminole, Choctaw, Creek, and Cherokee Nations. The creation of the commission had caused something of a land rush in the Territory, and within a year, the Indian was outnumbered four to one by the "intruder." The influx brought new situations, many that were violent in nature, and more work was generated for the deputy marshals. Many Indians bitterly opposed the concept of the Dawes Commission, quite correctly charging that the Indian way of life would disappear forever. In rebuttal were the existing conditions; the best lands in the Territory came under the control of a comparatively few Indians. Acquisition of land by newcomers for homes, even towns, was obtained by "renting" or "leasing" property from Indian owners. Often, the transactions were verbal. It was a situation that could breed ulcers for lawyers dealing with abstracts.

With the resistance of tribal governments to the Dawes Commission came further action from Washington. The commission was given more power to make up tribal rolls as a basis for allotment of lands. It was a gigantic task, and it called for more commissioners.

When the members of the Dawes Commission began riding the Nations, Bill and Jim Cook, and Cherokee Bill also took to the saddle. Their talents provided Walter "Spunky" Taylor with his first taste of life as a journeyman deputy marshal.

As a result of the opening of the famed Cherokee Outlet to homesteaders, the government prepared to make payments to the Indians for the strip of land. In June 1894, a huge sum of money was deposited with the Treasurer of the Cherokee Nation at Tahlequah. Each tribal member would receive $265 "strip money." Quite naturally, a large force of officers was on hand to guard the money, and make an attempt to oversee the conduct of the "newly rich." Tahlequah was filled with bunco artists of every description, eagerly awaiting the flow of money. The lawmen had a double chore.

The two Cook boys and Cherokee Bill were legally due their strip money, but they did not dare show their faces in Tahlequah. They figured out a means of getting their money. Seeking out a friend at Fourteen Mile Creek, about fifteen miles out of the Cherokee capital, they persuaded her to go into the town and present their written orders for the money. The woman agreed, and received the money, but of course the officers trailed her to Fourteen Mile Creek. A fierce gun battle followed, and one officer was killed. Jim

Cook was badly wounded and the beleaguered outlaws fled, but later the wounded outlaw was captured.

Receiving a harsh setback seemed to have spurred Bill Cook to reorganize. Possibly his rapidly changing homeland, which brought bitterness to many Cherokees, was a factor. At any rate, he formed a highly efficient gang.

Jim French, a handsome and dashing half-blooded Cherokee who had "trained" with the Belle Starr outfit, even sparking the Queen of the Outlaws, saw Bill Cook's professional touch and joined up. Others with equal daring were allowed membership. They were Thurman "Skeeter" Baldwin, Curtis Dayson, Jess "Buck" Snyder, Elmer "Chicken" Lucas, Sam "Verdigris Kid" McWilliams, George Sanders, Henry Munson, and Lon Gordon.

Deputy Marshals Paden Tolbert and Spunky Taylor received their full share of saddle work as a result of the activities of the Cook Gang. Much of the freebooters' daily activity consisted of chancing upon solitary riders in the Territory. The gang would relieve the unfortunate travelers of anything they deemed to be of value, except horses. The outlaws were already astride the choicest horseflesh, carefully selected nocturnally from the vast number of corrals in the Nations.

By the time outraged or thoroughly frightened travelers could register a protest and a description, the outlaws would be miles away. Still, the lawmen were forced to put in an appearance at the scene of a crime, and doggedly check for clues that were usually nonexistent.

The Cook Gang planned major projects with care. July 14, 1894, Bill Cook and his cohorts coolly and professionally held up the Tahlequah-Fort Gibson stagecoach. The startled driver tossed down the strongbox, and the shotgun guard sat with his hands helplessly reaching skyward. Profane orders quickly ejected the passengers, who hastily forked over their valuables to the hard-bitten gang. While deputy marshals were studying the site for clues, the gang struck again two days later, holding up a Frisco train near Tulsey Town.

But if the mode of outlawry was viciously changing, so was the attitude of many settlers in the Territory. The tempo of the area was increasing, for the Dawes Commission was at work. Even the Indians were aware, though most would not admit the fact even to themselves, that the old way of life in the Territory was coming to an end. With their mores at stake, the Indians had little time or patience with maverick members of tribes. The greatest asset the outlaw had in the Nations was rupturing—he could no longer depend entirely on folks refusing to aid the law. The grim persistence of the professional lawmen won admiration from people who themselves knew what was required to reach goals in an often savage land.

Deputy Marshal Paden Tolbert received a tip that three members of the Cook Gang were planning to "case" the town of Catoosa for some nefarious purpose. As the tip came from a reliable source, and since Spunky Taylor was familiar with the town, the two lawmen set out for the wild cattle-shipping little metropolis.

Arriving at the edge of town, the two deputy marshals pulled up in front of the stage stop at the old fort site. A restaurant located there was held in good repute by trailmen. Thinking they were well in advance of the three Cook Gang members, Tolbert and Taylor decided to stow away a square meal before entering the town. Inside the restaurant, the lawmen noticed a large sign on the counter that advertised a large meal for two bits.

Upon completion of their meal, Spunky Taylor flipped a fifty-cent piece on the counter.

"The bill is a dollar and a quarter," stated the restaurant keeper blandly.

"How come," requested the astounded Taylor, glancing at the big sign on the counter.

"Well," replied the restaurant man, "them three fellers,

what et just before you'uns come in, said their two buddies
back down the trail would be along in a few minutes and
pay for their grub. I knowed they was 'laws,' cause they
had Colts and Winchesters just like yourn."

Paying the bill, the grim-eyed lawmen stalked out of the
restaurant. But soon, they were overcome with mirth at the
idea of feeding three of the Cook bunch.

"If Charley Copeland finds out about this," said Tolbert,
wiping his eyes, "I'll never heah the last of it!"

Shortly thereafter, the wily Cook Gang struck in a locale
far removed from the Catoosa area.

On August 31, the hard-riding Cook bunch slipped over
into the Oklahoma Territory and held up the Lincoln
County Bank at the town of Chandler. Disgorging the safe
of $3000, they galloped madly out of town, shooting down a
barber who had rushed out of his shop to holler an alarm.
The first casualty for the gang resulted from that holdup.
A hastily organized posse, pounding in pursuit, managed to
get close enough to shoot Chicken Lucas out of his saddle.
The remainder of the gang reached wooded country and
escaped, leaving the wounded Lucas to be captured.

October 10, 1894, the Cook Gang raided the Missouri
Pacific depot at Claremore. Deputy Marshals Tolbert and
Taylor were only a couple of hours ride distant, and they
received the unwelcome news. Putting their mounts to hard
gallops, they arrived at the holdup site with the horses
lathered and blowing. A telegram was waiting for them.
The Cook Gang had held up the Katy depot at Choteau,
twenty miles away!

On October 20, Deputy Marshals Heck Bruner and Jose
Casaver, along with two railroad company detectives, were
riding guard on the Kansas City-Missouri Pacific express
when the Cook Gang held it up. The bandits effectively
stopped the train by throwing a switch on a siding about
five miles south of Wagoner. When his locomotive lurched
on the switch and headed down the siding, the engineer

quickly manipulated his levers. The big drivers of the engine pounded in reverse, but the train had enough momentum to ram a string of empty cars at the end of the siding with considerable force. A number of passengers were catapulted from their seats, and there was much confusion and shouting.

Before the dust of the jolting stop had settled, occupants of the train found themselves menaced by outlaw guns. Two gang members captured the engineer and fireman, and led them back to the baggage and express car. A salvo of hot lead drummed against the wooden car, and in answer to shouted commands, the agents opened the big doors. Meanwhile, more gang members were maintaining an accurate barrage to discourage anyone attempting to leave the stalled train. Bandits in the passenger coaches were resorting to the Jesse James trick of extracting valuables from the travelers.

The smooth operation was suddenly interrupted. The distant hoot of an approaching train caused Bill Cook, who was superintending operations from a loading platform at the siding, to shout for a general retreat. Bill was not taking chances that the oncoming train would turn out to be a string of flatcars loaded with lawmen.

The departing gang leveled a hail of bullets at the coaches, shattering every window. One passenger was seriously wounded, others received cuts from flying shards of glass. When the shots, and sounds of horses' hoofs diminished, the trainmen took stock. It was decided to back the riddled train to Wagoner in order to secure medical aid for the wounded man.

The railroad companies operating in the Territory changed their schedules as much as possible to eliminate night runs. Railroad men could understand the timing and organization that was behind the acts of the Cook Gang. Cherokee Bill however, began to emerge as a separate

entity. His deeds were not planned. The dark, loutish outlaw responded to the dictates of a ferocious nature.

November 9, 1894, the Cook Gang held up the Schufeldt
store in Lenapah with its usual aplomb. The bandits completed their mission, and were mounted, ready to dash
away. Cherokee Bill suddenly decided he needed a fresh
supply of ammunition, which no doubt he did, considering
the recently riddled train. Dismounting, the big outlaw
swaggered back into the store and demanded a few boxes
of .44-40 cartridges. As he was tucking his loot under his
arm, Bill happened to glance out a store window. Across a
vacant lot, a face was peering from a restaurant window.
Bill raised his Winchester with one hand and expertly fired
at the target in the window. Ernest Melton slumped to the
floor of the restaurant with a bullet in his head. Calmly
remounting, and ignoring the furious gaze of Bill Cook,
Cherokee Bill followed the gang out of town.

The senseless murder of the Lenapah citizen enraged
Territorial people more than the repetitious holdups. The
breach between outlaws and honest folks was widening.
The railroad companies faced the problem of having enough
guards aboard a train, but not great enough numbers to
"kill" business. Passengers and shippers of goods were becoming nervous.

With the call out for efficient guards to serve on trains
in the Territory, Deputy Sheriff Bud Ledbetter of Johnson
County believed that his services would be of more benefit
in the Nations. In July 1894, the big lawman moved to the
Territory and had no difficulty signing up as a Wells Fargo
guard. The paths of Bud Ledbetter and Paden Tolbert
crossed November 13, when they were assigned as guards
for a huge payroll aboard the Katy Flyer, bound for
Kansas City. Two other guards were also on duty in the
express coach, and the two Johnson County men were relat-
ing their experiences since they had last seen each other,
when the train swayed and came to a grinding halt.

Nathaniel "Texas Jack" Reed and his gang of three men had struck. The lure was the huge amount of money in the express coach strongbox. The outlaws had selected the Blackstone Switch, north of Muskogee a few miles, as an ideal spot to hijack a train. Utilizing a Bill Cook method, Texas Jack had thrown a switch, diverting the train from the mainline to the siding. However, the engineer was able to get his locomotive stopped before a crash occurred.

The lawmen in the baggage and express car calmly locked the large side doors, guessing what had caused the unscheduled stop. While one of the outlaws banged away at the express car, first on one side and then the other, passengers in the coaches were being robbed by the other two bandits. Soon the two in the coaches completed their chore and joined the third one at the express car. The lawmen ignored the bullets that thumped through the wooden walls, and they were silent to shouted demands to "open up, or be dynamited."

Texas Jack had neither the time or patience to palaver; he hurled a bundle of explosives. The blast splintered one end of the coach, and through the jagged opening thus provided, Bud Ledbetter spied the outlaw leader. Ledbetter quickly levered a rifle ball through the bandit's kidneys.

Seriously wounded, Texas Jack called his cohorts together. The leader had lost his gold fever, and his gang members could not proceed without a captain. Texas Jack was helped aboard his horse, and then it was every man for himself. Hiding out, the gang leader suffered the tortures of the damned, and he desperately conceived an idea. He sent word to Fort Smith that he would surrender in exchange for clemency, to be granted by Texas Jack turning state's evidence and revealing the "brains" behind a particular wave of train holdups. The outlaw's proposition was accepted, and he named Jim Dyer as the real head of the holdup artists. The famous Dyer case was precipitated in Judge Parker's court, but Dyer eventually was able to clear himself.

By a congressional act of March 1, 1895, three Federal Districts were created in the Indian Territory; the Northern, Central, and Southern. The Northern District had headquarters in Muskogee, which had boasted a United States Court since 1889. Morton Rutherford was appointed U. S. Marshal at Muskogee, and he wanted experienced men. He prevailed upon a number of veteran deputies to transfer to the new District. One of the deputies was Paden Tolbert, who bought a house in the town of Vinita. Moving to the same frontier town were G. S. White and Heck Bruner. Bill Smith, Dave Rusk, Enos Mills, Tom Johnson, and Charley Copeland also became familiar figures in the town.

With a mother's sensitivity to danger, Lizzie Tolbert naturally had concern for her children when J. R. Tolbert had proposed moving his family from Georgia to Johnson County, Arkansas, in 1880. Her innate fears were partially borne out May 4, 1895, when Charley Tolbert was seriously wounded.

Charley had an altercation with Will Watson, a former Negro employee, concerning wages. Watson cursed Tolbert, who leaped from his buggy and struck the Negro with the butt of a buggy whip. Watson then pulled a large knife and stabbed Tolbert, and fled the scene.

Deputy Marshal Paden Tolbert left for Clarksville immediately, and Charley died from his wound the following night. The efficient law of Johnson County, however, quickly apprehended Watson. Deputy Sheriffs King, Stephans, and May trailed the fugitive to the vicinity of Mulberry and captured him twelve hours after Charley Tolbert's death.

Lucy Tolbert's nerves were subjected to strain, in common with the wives of deputy marshals. Shortly after Paden Tolbert had brought his wife and baby daughter to the

new home in Vinita, he was trying out a frisky young mule
on a lonely road at the edge of town. Coming down the
road was a horseman armed with a rifle. It was one of the
rare times Paden Tolbert left his home without his firearms.
As luck would have it, Tolbert recognized the horseman as
a fugitive from the law.

As the two riders came abreast, Tolbert paused and
admired the "fine Winchester" the other was carrying. The
unsuspecting outlaw saw only a bronzed, heavy-set fellow
astride a mule, and he took him for an innocent farmer
who had pleasing, courteous manners. The outlaw obligingly
handed over the weapon upon Tolbert's polite hint that he
would like to "try the heft."

Tolbert eased the lever down enough to ascertain that a
yellow brass cartridge was in the chamber. Suddenly, the
outlaw was looking down the bore of his own gun, and a
cold, blue eye was staring at him over the gunsight. He
prudently accompanied Tolbert to town, and jail.

As time passed, Lucy Tolbert became better adjusted
to the surprises her husband's profession presented.

The United States Court at Muskogee was very active,
and Marshal Rutherford had his eye peeled at all times
for good lawmen. Felony cases could be tried in the court
at Muskogee, but murder cases required that the persons so
charged be brought to Parker's Court at Fort Smith. Still,
there was plenty of business, and admiring the cool nerve
of Bud Ledbetter that was displayed during the Blackstone
train robbery, Rutherford added the big, steely-eyed Ledbetter to his force June 25, 1895.

Paden Tolbert and his comrades continued the stint of
long hours in the saddle, chasing the light-footed Cook
Gang. The gang was now being closely pressed. Lon Gordon, Henry Munson, and Curtis Dayson were surrounded
in a house near Sapulpa. Foolishly refusing to give up,
Gordon and Munson lost their lives in the ensuing gun
battle. Wounded, Dayson was captured and reunited with

his friend Chicken Lucas in the Fort Smith jail. Judge Parker handed them stiff sentences in the penitentiary.

The Cook Gang began to come apart at the seams. Deciding to leave the Territory until conditions cooled, the worried bandits headed for Mexico, but the Texas Rangers grabbed Baldwin, Snyder, and Farris, and they were brought to Fort Smith. Bill Cook had managed to dodge that capture, and he turned his horse toward New Mexico. However, authorities had been alerted to watch for him, and he was soon captured near the site where Pat Garrett had gunned down Billy the Kid. Cook also was returned to Fort Smith where he was later sentenced by Judge Parker to a forty-five-year penitentiary term.

Jim French and Cherokee Bill parted company soon after. The handsome outlaw could not stomach the burly, fierce Cherokee Bill. The pair was cautiously proceeding down a trail one day, with the usual posse not too far behind. The outlaws chanced upon an Indian boy riding a skinny pony. Cherokee Bill decided that he wanted the pony.

Knowing that the psychopathic bandit intended to shoot the Indian lad, French demurred on the grounds that the ill-fed pony could not keep up with their fleet horses. Mulling this bit of wisdom, Cherokee Bill decided to shoot the Indian boy anyway. Again, French disapproved, charging that the killing would only enrage people, and make posses more determined than ever.

Intent on killing something, Cherokee Bill noticed the Indian boy's dog, standing nervously up the trail a ways. "I'll kill the damn dog, then," the big fellow snarled.

Thoroughly disgusted, French carefully explained that he believed the lawmen were close enough on their trail to hear gunfire. With the sound of a shot, the posse would head for them in a dead run.

Muttering dark epithets, Cherokee Bill reluctantly followed the departing French. The terrified Indian boy left in the opposite direction as fast as the emaciated pony could run.

Coming to a fork in the trail, French suddenly pulled off, and the surprised Cherokee Bill rode on past before he could rein in his horse. Wheeling his mount so that he could face French and demand an explanation, he received another surprise. French's six gun was leveled on him, and the big hammer of the Colt was back at full cock.

"Feller," snarled French, "we are parting company. Start riding, and get out of my sight!"

Cherokee Bill had no choice, for Jim French with a drawn and cocked six-shooter was bad medicine. Scowling savagely, the big outlaw put the spurs to his horse and vanished down the trail.

Jim French was not by nature a lone-wolf type of operator. With the Cook Gang shattered, he joined forces with a minor hoodlum and attempted to rob the J. C. Patton store at Catoosa. The pair forced the door of the establishment late at night, but they came face to face with the store manager and the nightwatchman. The manager and his night guard had heard that French was in town, and they were expecting trouble. The nightwatchman, armed with a shotgun, promptly discharged the weapon at French's buddy, blowing away his face.

French managed to execute a fast draw and shoot the manager, and get the drop on the watchman. The guard dropped his shotgun.

The store manager, fatally wounded, was swaying on his feet. French gave him a shove, and the man staggered backward against a cot that the watchman used, and sat down.

French turned aside to check on his sprawled friend, and the dying manager found a revolver under the pillow on the cot. Raising the gun with both hands, he used his last strength to fire two shots, both bullets striking French in the neck.

Badly wounded, French dropped his gun and staggered through the open door of the store. Dazedly, he mounted his horse and rode as far as the edge of town. Unable to stay in the saddle, he tumbled to the ground. Seeing a cabin nearby, he painfully crawled to it and managed to raise himself in order to grasp the door latch. Opening the door, he sprawled inside. The occupants were appalled at the sudden appearance of an apparition with blood spurting from its neck, and they fled for the town.

Among the townspeople drawn to the store by the sounds of gunfire in the night was Deputy Marshal Spunky Taylor. He learned that Jim French had shot the store manager and escaped. He was busily organizing a posse when the frightened man and his wife, who lived in the cabin at the edge of town, arrived on the scene with the news that a badly wounded man had broken into their house. Taylor and a crowd of townspeople rushed to the cabin.

Jim French had somehow managed to die with his boot jammed into the fireplace. The boot and a portion of the corpse's leg was burned away.

Deputy Marshal Bill Smith knew that Cherokee Bill had a grudge against him, but now that the savage outlaw was on the prowl without the backing of a gang, Smith did not believe that the killer was in the vicinity of his home at Nowata. Heck Bruner and a posse had closed in on Cherokee Bill near Tulsey Town. They shot the outlaw's horse out from under him, but the fierce breed escaped into nearby woods and soon had commandeered another horse. No one knew his whereabouts. However, Smith returned home after an absence of a few days on a case, and he found his wife and small daughter in a terrified state.

Cherokee Bill had appeared during the marshal's absence. He unlatched the front gate and rode into the yard. Slowly riding around the house, trampling flower beds, he peered fiercely at each window. Then, he rode away. Watching from behind barred doors and locked windows were Mrs. Smith and the little girl.

"Daddy," sobbed the child, "he was on a big, black horse, and he was big and black, and awfully mean-look-ing."

Bill Smith's black eyes grew hard as obsidian. He wasted no time.

Ike Rogers, a deputy marshal, had a cousin, Maggie Glass, with whom Cherokee Bill was infatuated. Smith promised Rogers a "fine Winchester" that he owned if he would arrange to have Maggie at Rogers' home, near Nowata, and get word out so that the outlaw would know that the girl was there. Rogers, knowing that the outlaw was sparking his cousin, had been feeling a considerable amount of guilt because he had been able to do nothing about the situation. Here was his chance. He enlisted the aid of his neighbor, Clint Scales, and the trap was set.

Maggie was suspicious, even though the outlaw had been known to Rogers for a long time. The idea of Cherokee Bill coming to the home of a deputy marshal just didn't sound right to Maggie. In due time, the trail-worn Cherokee Bill arrived, after having cased the premises for some time from concealment. Maggie attempted to pass along her fears, but Cherokee Bill would hear none of it. He had been on the scout for a long time, and it was good to sit in a chair, and contemplate a home-cooked meal. Also, the presence of his sweetheart served to dull the alarm bells for the tired outlaw.

The host was in rare good humor. Rogers announced that the event called for fried chicken, and he sent Maggie over to good neighbor Scales's house for a big fat hen. Scales, on the pretext that he would have to catch the hen, delivered the fowl in person in a short while. Rogers grandly invited neighbor Scales to remain and partake of the upcoming feast.

A restless night wore along after the big meal. The host and his neighbor chatted aimlessly on subjects of common interest, waiting for the surly outlaw to drop his guard. The burly breed kept his Winchester near his chair, and his outlaw life had long since made him as wary as a wild animal. Finally tiring of the unromantic atmosphere, Maggie left the room and went to bed. The outlaw contented himself playing solitaire while Rogers and Scales talked.

Finally, Cherokee Bill twisted a quirley from his sack of Bull Durham and leaned forward to extract an ember from the fireplace in order to light his smoke. Instantly, Rogers grabbed the poker and dealt the outlaw a blow on the head "that would have killed an ordinary man."

Knocked to his hands and knees, Cherokee Bill shook his head dazedly, and Rogers' wife snatched the outlaw's Winchester and left the room. Rogers and Scales leaped on Cherokee Bill, but the big outlaw stood erect with both men clinging to his neck. Fighting now for their lives, the two men wrestled furiously with the outlaw, and Rogers' modest furniture was knocked helter-skelter about the room. Finally, they managed to get handcuffs on first one wrist, and then the other of the infuriated Cherokee Bill. Leaping back, Rogers pantingly drew out his six gun and shouted for the outlaw to stand still.

Seeing that Rogers intended to shoot, Cherokee Bill ceased his struggles, and began begging to be set free. He succeeded only in making his two adversaries shudder. They did not even like to think of what would happen if the outlaw was suddenly freed.

Rogers and Scales quickly ushered Cherokee Bill outdoors and hitched a wagon to a team. With Scales driving, they set out for Nowata. Rogers followed closely on horseback. For a while, the manacled outlaw was still in the wagon bed. Perhaps he thought of meeting Judge Parker face to face. With a mighty grunt, he snapped the chain connecting the wrist gauntlets. He made a lunge for Scales' Winchester, but Scales threw himself backward out of the wagon. Rogers covered the outlaw until Scales got his breath back and climbed into the wagon. Scales and Rogers conferred. They decided to shoot the outlaw the very next move he made. It was just too dangerous attempting to deliver Cherokee Bill alive.

Having no desire to commit suicide, the sullen outlaw remained quiet for the remainder of the trip to Nowata. The prisoner was delivered to Deputy Marshals Bill Smith and George Lawson. Bill Smith kept his promise and presented Rogers with his best Winchester.

It was a long train ride to Fort Smith, and there were long legal steps to be made before Cherokee Bill would stand on the big gallows. The big outlaw still had some bloody history to enact.

14

TO THE LAST OUTLAW GANG

News of the capture of Cherokee Bill spread with the speed of a prairie grass fire across the Indian Territory. A railroad company jubilantly offered the use of a locomotive and caboose to transport the outlaw to Fort Smith, and Deputy Marshal Bill Smith accepted the offer. Deputy George Lawson recruited Ike Rogers and Clint Scales to serve as extra guards.

Bill Smith attached heavy shackles to the outlaw's ankles, and when he ordered his prisoner to enter the caboose, Cherokee Bill had a difficult time hobbling up the steep steps. Smith grimly pointed to a seat in the center of the little car, and without argument the outlaw seated himself. Telegraphic messages preceded the little locomotive and its swaying single caboose, and when the stop at Wagoner was made, the entire population was on hand to cheer the lawmen.

The noisy crowd clamored for a view of the outlaw; they wanted to see him in chains. Knowing that the people were justified in their jubilation, and their desire to see "The Terror" in chains, the marshals brought the outlaw down to the station platform. With an audience of large proportions to face, the sullen Cherokee Bill became bold and cocky. A photographer, with his huge camera and folded tripod, asked the lawmen for permission to take a picture. Again, the marshals did not have the heart to refuse.

The photographer arranged his subjects with the outlaw in the center of the group of marshals. The happy crowd was finally shoved out of range of the camera lens, and the bright day offered plenty of light for the picture. At the urging of the photographer, all eyes of the subjects were on his waving hand as he prepared to squeeze his shutter bulb.

Cherokee Bill, with a great show of bravado, put his arm around the shoulders of the marshal standing on his right. As the photographer called for his subjects to "watch the birdie," the outlaw slyly reached for the lawman's holstered revolver. Fortunately, a pair of sharp eyes in the crowd spotted the move. A shouted warning caused the lawman to twist away. Bill Smith placed a guard behind the outlaw, and the picture was made. The outlaw was then hustled aboard the train, and the cheers of the crowd were drowned by the shriek of the locomotive whistle as it triumphantly pulled the caboose away from the Wagoner station. Under the hard eyes of Bill Smith, the dangerous prisoner was forced to sit quietly, and the remainder of the trip to Fort Smith was uneventful. Ike Rogers and Clint Scales heaved sighs of relief as the heavy doors of the Fort Smith jail clanged shut on Cherokee Bill.

Judge Parker wasted no time in convicting Cherokee Bill of the murder of Ernest Melton at Lenapah. However, appeals were being made from Parker's sentences. The outlaw's attorneys gained a stay of execution, and during that time nearly 250 prisoners in the Fort Smith jail were in a restless mood. Jailers knew that some kind of revolt was brewing, and their diligence resulted in the finding of a revolver in the jail washroom. It had been smuggled inside in a bucket of lime that was to be used for antiseptic cleaning. The officers did not know at the time that a second six-shooter had been smuggled into Cherokee Bill's cell.

The wily outlaw hid his treasure cleverly. He pried a brick loose and broke off all but the facing. He then secreted the gun in the aperture and replaced the brick facing. It was a foolproof job of hiding a gun.

July 26, 1895, guards Lawrence Keating and Campbell Eoff were making their rounds, routinely checking cell locks. They found the lock on a cell to be faulty. The cell contained a half-witted prisoner, situated next to the cell that held Cherokee Bill. The lock mechanism of the half-wit's cell door was stuffed with wadded newspaper. The guards paused and were examining the jammed lock, when Cherokee Bill shoved his six-shooter through his cell bars and pressed it against Keating's stomach.

"Gimme them damn keys!" the outlaw snarled.

Cherokee Bill's move caught the guard by surprise. Keating knew that if he pulled the key from the jammed lock and handed the ring of keys to the outlaw, some 250 prisoners would be loosed on Fort Smith. Keating went for his gun.

Before the guard's six gun cleared leather, the outlaw squeezed the trigger of his weapon. It was point-black range, and the shock of the heavy .45 left Keating with no chance of life. He staggered to the end of the cell row and fell dead.

Campbell Eoff, frantically attempting to jerk the key from the jammed lock, gave up and ducked behind a door in order to save his life as Cherokee Bill fired four shots at him.

The full scope of the jail-break plot was never discovered. Evidently, Cherokee Bill had been taken into the plans, for the plotters knew that he could be depended upon to make the initial move, even killing, if necessary. It was believed that George Pierce, one of the prisoners, was a chief plotter. When Pierce saw Eoff dive behind the door, he thought the guard was carrying the jail keys. Arming himself by smashing a small table against the brick wall of his cell, Pierce secured a stout leg of the ruined table. With the table leg in his fist, Pierce lunged from his cell, seeking

Eoff. Deputy Marshal George Lawson appearing at the far end of the jail floor, ruined whatever plans Pierce had. The marshal began firing and forced Pierce back into his cell, which was in a row that had not yet been locked by the guards.

Cherokee Bill was hastily reloading his gun, but before he could menace Lawson, a crashing of boots on the stairs diverted his attention. Alerted by the racket of gunfire, guards Will Lawson, Bras Parker, Tom Parker and Will Mc-Connell, the brother of Bud McConnell, appeared on the scene. They were immediately followed by Head Jailer J. D. Berry and Deputy Marshal Heck Bruner. A hot sniping match began, and the jail floor was quickly filled with the stinging fumes of gun smoke. Most of the prisoners huddled, terrified, in their cells.

Cherokee Bill gave the blood-curdling death gobble of the Cherokee, and outlaw Henry Starr, who happened to be a guest of Judge Parker's at the time, shouted something in the language of the Cherokees. Whatever the words were that Starr uttered, Cherokee Bill yielded, tossing his hot pistol out of his cell. The glowering outlaw refused to divulge any information concerning the jail-break attempt. The guards chained him to the wall of his cell by means of ankle shackles.

Meanwhile, on the grounds below, a huge crowd had been attracted by the brief but furious cannonade inside the jail walls. Upon learning that Lawrence Keating had been murdered by Cherokee Bill, the crowd became ugly. Keating, a married man with children, was held in high esteem by Fort Smithians. A surge for a lynching was forming as Marshal Crump, his trousers and coat pulled hastily over his night clothes, arrived to take charge. The marshal perceived that the crowd would shortly become a dangerous mob unless checked. He ordered all available deputy marshals to mingle in the crowd and preserve order.

One of the deputies was Paden Tolbert, who was in Fort

Smith to testify in the trial of Cherokee Bill. Tolbert strolled calmly among the throngs. Encountering a hothead shouting for a lynching, he would order the fellow to subside or become a guest in a jail cell. Many in the crowd were persons with whom Tolbert was acquainted. He paused for a few minutes at first one group and then another.

"Think it over," he would remark, "breaking the law won't fix anything. Besides, it's dangerous—some of you know better. Rush that jail, and a bunch of you will get hurt. Judge Parker will take care of Cherokee Bill."

However, as is the usual case when an angry crowd convenes, there were erratic individuals scattered throughout the huge throng.

"Kind of an exciting night," Tolbert drawled, as he chanced upon a fellow deputy, Isaac Greenbury "Mike" Mahan.

Mike Mahan, with a reputation for mildness that rivaled Paden Tolbert's mien, nodded in agreement. Then, the excited actions of three husky young men caught his eye.

"Here, here, now," Marshal Mahan remonstrated as he stepped over to the men. He grasped the arm of one who was in the act of hurling a brick at a glass window of the courtroom. "Let's cool down a little."

The wild-eyed young man turned his head to see who dared lay a hand on his throwing arm.

Mike Mahan stood six feet five inches in height, and he weighed 250 pounds. He stared down, with his mild blue eyes, into the flushed face of the man with the brick. The fellow had seen Mahan around Fort Smith for a number of years, and he considered the marshal to be a big ox who was so good-natured that he went around town humming gay little tunes to himself.

"By gawd—" began the red-faced man, but he was unable to finish his sentence. Sadly, the big marshal tightened his grip on the fellow's arm, and the brick slipped from nerveless fingers and thudded on the ground.

"Now, sonny," said the marshal, "I would just as soon you'd get with your friends over there and keep your mouth shut."

With a sweeping motion of his ponderous arm, Mahan flung the hapless man with the white, pain-twisted face, head on into the midriffs of his two friends. The two were bowled over by the hurtling figure. Picking themselves up, the three studied the hulking form of the marshal for a moment, and then they slunk away into the crowd. They had lost interest in drumming up a lynching.

Paden Tolbert could not suppress a grin, despite the gravity of the situation. Mike Mahan, along with his giant physique, was famed as an expert fiddler. Mahan had long admired a Stradivarius violin owned by an aged music teacher. Sensing the huge fellow's love for the fine old instrument, the teacher often permitted the marshal to play it. One day, a sudden fire swept through the building where the teacher conducted his music classes. The old fellow was unable to escape, but he managed to fling his precious Stradivarius out of a window. Authorities, unable to find any trace of heirs, gave the valuable instrument to the big deputy marshal.

"By daylight," Tolbert mused, "the whole town will know that the good-natured fiddler can get his dander up."

The firm presence of Parker's lawmen successfully kept the crowd under control. In the dawn hours, everybody became chilled, and the unreasoning anger vanished. The crowd slowly dwindled away.

Once again Cherokee Bill came to trial. Beginning August 8, 1895, he was tried for the murder of Lawrence Keating. The trial lasted three days, and the now famous outlaw's record was reviewed. It was never even attempted in the court to prove how many people Cherokee Bill had slain. Rumors placed the figure at thirty.

The court was concerned only with the slaying of Keating, and the jury was out only thirteen minutes. Judge Parker set the sentence of hanging for September 10. Again, an effort on the part of the outlaw's lawyer resulted in a stay of execution, but this time, an appeal was turned down. Parker reset the hanging for March 17, 1896. Only Presidential pardon could save the blood-thirsty Cherokee Bill, and such a pardon was not forthcoming.

The husky outlaw met his fate with considerable calmness. It was a St. Patrick's Day Fort Smithians long remembered. While standing on the trap door of the gallows, Cherokee Bill made his purported reply to requests for last words:

"I came here to die, not to make a speech!"

The folks in the Indian Territory breathed a sigh of relief.

Although the deputy marshals had no way of knowing the fact at the time, when Cherokee Bill plunged through the well-worn trap door of the gray old gallows, he was the last of the well-publicized outlaws to be stayed by the hand of justice while at the peak of his black profession.

However, the old gallows had a few more chores of chastisement to perform. Eight more felons would stand on the trap door before history could tally up Judge Parker's total of seventy-nine hangings.

As though to protest the bowing out of the outlaw breed, the savage Buck Gang appeared for a brief frenzy of crime in the Indian Territory. But the Buck Gang was not rated in the outlaw category by lawmen. They considered the motley crew on the level of mad dogs, to be hunted down and killed as quickly as possible. In a spree that lasted only thirteen days, the crude Buck Gang aroused the rage of the entire Territory.

Rufus Buck, a Euchee Indian, was the leader of the gang that bore his name. Maoma July and Sam Sampson were Creek outlaws, and Lucky and Lewis Davis were freedmen. The five men were no novices at breaking the law; they had served sentences at Fort Smith. They deliberately formed the union that came to be known as the Buck Gang.

July 28, 1895, they shot and killed Marshal John Garrett because the crack officer, not liking their looks, was watching their movements. Temporarily free of surveillance, but necessarily on the scout, the gang fled to remote districts.

The Buck Gang was not long in coming across its next victim, a widow driving a wagonload of her household goods. The gang was not interested in the contents of the wagon. They accosted the woman, and each had his way with her. The gang rode away, leaving the unfortunate woman in hysterics.

In a short time the Buck outfit chanced upon another woman, riding horseback alone. The sadistic group again violated the pristine code of the Territory. Women were not harmed by the professional outlaws, and molestation of women was a charge the deputy marshals seldom encountered. The Buck Gang subjected the horsewoman to the same ordeal they had inflicted on the widow. They discarded her sidesaddle and led her horse away, leaving her beside the trail.

The next victim was a man, traveling alone on horseback. They stripped the traveler of everything he owned, even his clothing. Rufus Buck had no other thought than killing the victim, but others of the gang were enjoying their seeming power over life and death. They wanted to hold a vote. A vote was then taken, and oddly enough, the nays outnumbered the yeas. The violent crew rode away, leaving the terrified but relieved traveler shivering in his birthday suit.

The horses of the Buck Gang were now played out by the fast, erratic moves of the outfit. They sought new mounts and descended upon the ranch of Gus Chambers on Duck Creek. Chambers owned a fine herd of thoroughbred horses, and he was a man with plenty of courage. He stood off the gang from his house, using a shotgun that was capable of reaching, and protecting, his corral of valuable livestock. The Buck Gang did not have the courage for a fight where they could be hurt. They angrily riddled the rancher's house with rifle lead from a safe distance, and rode away to seek a less presumptuous victim.

The gang swooped down on Benton Callahan and one of his cowboys, catching them completely by surprise. Callahan owned the U-Bar Ranch, situated near Checotah, and the pair was driving a herd of stock. The cowboy's horse was shot from under him, and as the grounded man attempted to reach the safety of the brush beside the trail, the outlaws calmly dropped him in his tracks. Callahan was wounded on the side of his head, and the gang secured the stock they were after. They rode away, permitting Callahan to live.

The gang next appeared at the home of Henry Hassan, who owned a small spread southeast of Tulsey Town, in the Creek Nation. Rufus Buck had once had an argument with Hassan concerning points of the Creek tribal law, and he bore a grudge against the rancher. However, Buck was not noted for his interest in law; he knew that Rosetta Hassan, Henry Hassan's wife, was an extremely attractive woman.

The motley group overpowered the suprised Hassan before he could reach his Winchester. The outlaws then profanely ordered the frightened couple to prepare a huge meal. Well fed, the gang set up a vicious tableau. One by one, they assaulted Mrs. Hassan, forcing the bound Hassan to observe by pressing six guns to each temple. Then, they amused themselves by making Hassan and his hired hand, who had been captured in the barn, wrestle in a mudhole. The gang kept up a barrage of gunfire at the two victims' feet in order to elicit action.

Soon the sport palled for the outlaws, and their ammunition was running low. They rode away in search of new victims. Selecting remote spots, they robbed the Red Store at Norberg and Orcutt's store at the hamlet of McDermott.

With their load of ammunition, food supplies, and baubles, they fled to a nearby knoll to sort out the valuables.

The populace of the Indian Territory was virtually up in arms. The Creek Lighthorse, under the leadership of Harry Edmond, had its ranks swelled by nearly a hundred irate citizens. Marshal Morton Rutherford at Muskogee dispatched Deputy Marshals Frank Jones, Paden Tolbert, Bud Ledbetter, N. B. Irwin, and Sam Haynes.

The federal men put in two days, with little sleep, chasing clues and rumors, but it was the Lighthorse that came upon the Buck Gang.

The experienced Indian police had difficulty with members of the posse. Angry men wanted to storm up the hill and take the gang by brute force immediately. The outlaws had the advantage of the terrain. Hiding in the tall grass atop their knoll, they presented poor targets for the posse. The posse was not concerned with minor difficulties; they quickly surrounded the base of the hill, and the outlaws had no recourse. They began fighting for their lives. During each lull, a number of the possemen would advance a little further up the hill.

Paden Tolbert and Bud Ledbetter, with their fellow deputy marshals, heard the rattle of gunfire in the distance. It did not take the federal men long to arrive at the scene of the battle. A ricochet bullet clipped Rufus Buck's belt, and his sagging pants completed the demoralization that had begun when the outlaw saw that he would have to fight for his life. Buck bolted down the slope, his only thought to escape, and he intended leaving his buddies to face the enraged posse. He didn't get ten feet. He ran headlong into the newly arrived marshals, and they promptly snapped cuffs on his wrists. At the same moment, the lawmen swarmed over the top of the hill and roughly disarmed the outlaws. The angered Creek tribesmen in the posse were all for stringing up the outlaws immediately. With considerable difficulty, and with a show of stubborn determination, the federal men were able to transport the cowed Buck Gang to Muskogee.

In a few hours the streets of Muskogee were filled with sullen, muttering men. They were converging on the jail, and Marshal Rutherford knew that a lynching was not far off. Climbing on top of a box, the marshal addressed the throng in the street, telling them that Judge Parker at Fort Smith would deal out justice legally. Rutherford was not getting through to the crowd, and he knew it. As he stepped down from his box, his calm features did not betray his worried thoughts.

Pleasant Porter, a prominent Creek figure, saved the day, for the time being. He heaved his portly frame atop Rutherford's box and raised his arms. The throng finally fell silent, and Porter pointed toward the jail. In the language of the Creeks, he said, "Friends, don't you see who is guarding the jail doors?"

All eyes followed Porter's pointing finger. Paden Tolbert and Bud Ledbetter, their Winchesters cradled in their arms, stood wide-legged in front of the thick jail door.

"You know," Porter stated to the crowd simply, "that if you rush that jail, some of you will die!"

The immediate danger passed. However, a large number of Creeks pitched camp near the jail, indicating that they were not fully convinced they should allow the Buck Gang to be taken away. Marshal Rutherford held a conference with his deputies, and a plan was quickly formulated. When darkness settled over the area, the lawmen issued a cool ultimatum to the outlaws. They were to pick up their leg chains gently, and quietly follow the marshals out the back door. Or they could make a slight noise and get lynched. The Buck Gang co-operated wholeheartedly, and before long, the thugs were jailed in Fort Smith.

The trial of the Buck Gang was a hectic affair, and complete with tense drama. Rosetta Hassan bravely agreed to testify, and volunteers appeared from the Territory who offered eye witness testimony against the outlaws. There was no lack of evidence, and the sordid details of the crimes the Buck Gang perpetrated soon had Judge Parker livid with rage. With his huge vocabulary, he thundered a blistering edict to the jury, which was out of the courtroom only three minutes. The Judge then sentenced the five felons to die simultaneously on the big gallows. On July 1, 1896, the trap door fell away under their feet.

The brief appearance of the Buck Gang rounded out the record in the Indian Territory. Every conceivable type of outlaw had flourished, and had been vanquished. The frontier setting and the nineteenth-century gunslinging outlaw were vanishing. The Territory was changing, and the hard core of Parker's men knew that some day, the "wild days" would come to an end. The lawmen no doubt sensed that there would be no sudden line of demarcation to indicate when lawlessness ceased, and they certainly never expressed a belief that there would be total peace some day in the field of law enforcement. They only knew that they had quelled the enormous tidal wave of crime in the Nations. The swells following the agitation of the big wave would undulate for some time.

The Parker Era, however, ended abruptly.

The tremendous load of work Judge Parker had been carrying for twenty-one years suddenly began exacting its toll. The big jurist fell ill. Dropsy, strain, overwork, and general exhaustion was the verdict of physicians. In order to prevent work from piling up in the fast-moving court, an alternate judge was placed on Parker's bench, and during this period Congress abolished the huge jurisdiction of the Fort Smith court. The Indian Territory was placed under the jurisdictions of the Federal Districts in the Nations.

November 17, 1896, ailing Judge Isaac C. Parker died at the age of fifty-eight. Keenly feeling the passing of the famous judge, Fort Smithians conducted a large funeral, and prominent figures made speeches. Parker was buried in the

Federal Cemetery near his court chambers. The Indians' silent anguish at the loss of a real friend was exemplified by Pleasant Porter. Without oratory, and representing all the Civilized Tribes, he placed a wreath of wild flowers on Parker's grave.

An iron pot with boiling contents will simmer long after the fire underneath it is extinguished. The day of the outlaw was waning, but a few of the "wild bunch" did not want to face the fact. The year following the death of Judge Parker, another Territorial outlaw challenged the might of law enforcement men.

Al Jennings was a lawyer at Woodward, in the Nations. He had a courtroom altercation with Temple Houston, the lawyer son of Texas hero Sam Houston. In a dramatic courtroom setting, Houston fast drew and killed Ed Jennings, a brother of Al Jennings. Houston was absolved of blame, and Al, along with his other brother, Frank, became incensed. They figured that society favored famous people.

Al Jennings became the epitome of the "last ditch" stand of Territorial outlaws. He attempted to pattern his career of crime after Jesse and Frank James in their heyday. The James outfit made elaborate plans to loot two banks simultaneously in 1876. Northfield, Minnesota, far from their home range, was the scene of their ambitious attempt. Citizens of the town rallied and poured a withering barrage of gunfire into the ranks of the freebooters. The two James boys barely escaped, but the Younger brothers were captured.

The 1892 plans of the Dalton Gang to loot two banks at Coffeyville, Kansas, was a planned, direct imitation of the James's method. The Daltons vowed they were going to "outdo the King of the Holdup Artists." The fate of the Daltons was strangely identical to that of the Jesse James Gang. Coffeyville citizens shot the gang to doll ribbons.

Escaping the fiasco at Coffeyville, gang member Bill Doolin soon formed his own violent group, terrorizing the Oklahoma Territory with daring but well-planned assaults. Lawmen, over a period of years, chopped the gang down. In 1896, Doolin was captured in a bathhouse at Eureka Springs, Arkansas, by Deputy Marshal Bill Tilghman, who was a veteran of Dodge City, Kansas, and a recipient of Ned Buntline's prodigious barreled "Buntline Colts." Doolin staged a jail break and was trailed for six weeks. Deputy Marshal Heck Thomas finally cornered him, and Doolin chose to ignore a chance to surrender. He died suddenly.

"Little Dick" West became the last free member of the Doolin Gang by virtue of fleeing the Territory. Eventually, the wizened little outlaw returned in time to find potential gang-member material in Al and Frank Jennings. A gang was formed, with Dick West as the leader. Along with the Jennings boys, Pat and Morris O'Malley were recruited, and the gang began operations in 1897.

The first attempt at outlawry was a train holdup at Edmond, but Dick West's men were inexperienced. They bungled the job so badly that their nerve broke, and they fled in confusion. But they were a determined gang and so they tackled a Katy train south of Muskogee, at Bond Switch. The gang utilized a stack of railroad ties that were stacked near the tracks. With considerable muscle strain, they piled the heavy timbers on the track. On schedule, the train approached, and the engineer spied the obstruction. He had been piloting locomotives in the Territory for some time and knew immediately that a holdup was being planned for his train. He jerked his throttle wide open. Thundering down the tracks at an earth-shaking pace, the iron giant plowed into the pile of heavy ties and scattered them as though they were jacksticks.

Becoming angry and dangerous, the frustrated gang "cased" the station at Purcell in order to figure out some way of looting the railroad. Their dark thoughts were reflected in their mannerisms, and the station agent became suspicious. He called for a squad of lawmen to guard the station. Thwarted, the West Gang slipped away.

Dick West, who had ridden for masters in the art of banditry, was becoming worried about his cronies and their future. He devised a method to stop a train in the open countryside, and on October 1, 1897, the gang found the ideal setup. A group of section hands were at work on the Rock Island tracks a few miles north of Chickasha. The gang swooped down on the workers and covered them with six guns. When the next train came along, the rail workers were forced to flag it down. With an express car strongbox at hand, the swaggering Al Jennings took over. He applied a large charge of dynamite. The poorly placed explosive wrecked the car, but left the safe unharmed. Confusion arose, and the trainmen began to mutter belligerently. The West Gang fled in angry frustration. Soon, a posse was dogging their trail, and Little Dick West was fed up with his crew. He walked out. In a short time West was tracked down and killed. Lawmen scratched the name of another troublemaker off the diminishing list.

Al Jennings made no secret of his admiration for the famous Jesse James. He was an avid reader of dime novels dealing with outlaw gangs, and he made the open boast that he could outdo the Dalton and Doolin bunch. All he had to do was to avoid the mistakes they made, and he announced himself the leader of the new Jennings Gang.

The town of Cushing had the honor of being selected by Al Jennings as his first port of call. The gang robbed a store, obtaining forty dollars and articles of clothing. Jennings, flushed with the mild success, was gleeful when posters popped up all over the Territory, offering a reward for the apprehension of the Jennings Gang. He figured that he was now "somebody."

If Al Jennings had read the case histories of the outlaw gangs of the Indian Territory as avidly as he perused fictional stories, he would have realized the reason for reward posters bearing his name appearing in so incredibly a short time. Harboring and protecting outlaws was no longer a custom in the Nations. The marshals no longer ferreted for days in search of hoofprints. If people had information, after seeing the posters, they would hunt up the lawmen.

In a short time, the Jennings Gang was sighted near Tulsey Town. They had paused at a blacksmith shop. Whether they were reconnoitering for a planned holdup, or seeking to have a horse shod, made little difference. They were forced to flee immediately to escape an oncoming posse. However, the determined Al paused long enough at Foyil to direct a robbery of the post office when the gang passed through that locale.

The last month of the year 1897 was at hand when the Jennings Gang was put out of commission. Whatever methods Al Jennings planned to use in order to "outdo" Jesse James will never be known. Deputy marshals were never far down the trail from the weary gang, and when the bushed outlaws holed up at the Spike S Ranch, sixteen miles south of Tulsey Town, the site was quickly surrounded.

In the cordon of lawmen were Paden Tolbert, Bud Ledbetter, Lon Lewis, Joe and Gus Thompson, John McClanahan, and Jake Elliot. The seasoned officers waited until dawn and then went to work. They found one of the O'Malley boys asleep in the bed of a wagon near the ranch house. He had been posted as a sentry by the canny Al.

Bud Ledbetter clamped a big hand over the mouth of the "sentry," and carried him into the barn. He was expertly trussed up and gagged. Lewis and Ledbetter took stations behind the barn. Tolbert crouched behind a stone chimney, relic of an earlier ranch house that had burned. Joe and Gus Thompson concealed themselves in nearby thickets while Elliot and McClanahan took positions behind a stone wall.

In a short time Clarence Enscoe came out of the ranch house to begin his day's chores by feeding the stock. When he entered the barn, Ledbetter and Lewis overpowered him and stretched him out beside O'Malley. The prolonged absence of Enscoe brought results. He was a brother of Mrs. John Harless, who managed the ranch, and she popped out of the house and ran to the barn to see what was delaying her brother. Confronted by Ledbetter, she had no choice except to listen to the big lawman's instructions.

"Tell the Jennings bunch to come out, we have them surrounded," Ledbetter stated, "and if they refuse, you, and anyone else in that house that want to keep away from bullets must get out."

Mrs. Harless returned to the house with the message. Redheaded Al Jennings shouted that he would "rather die first."

To the credit of Al Jennings, he made no attempt to hold Mrs. Harless, or a hired girl who was in the house, as hostages. The two women, leading a small boy, quickly left the house.

The gunfire commenced at once, and the outlaws desperately pumped answering shots as rapidly as they could. Tolbert, from his post behind the old chimney, received an eyeful of lime as a bullet caromed off one of the stones, dislodging the mortar. With the ease of long practice, the lawmen riddled the house. Clapboards splintered under the onslaught of Winchester slugs, and the bark of heavy six guns echoed to the sounds of smashing crockery, as utensils on the kitchen table dissolved into shards of broken earthenware.

All three of the outlaws received flesh wounds, and desperately, they dived from a back window of the house. With astonishing luck, they managed to reach the thickets and vanish before a hail of bullets could reach them. Later, the outlaws commandeered a wagon and team, but the marshals outguessed them.

Figuring that the Jennings bunch would attempt to flee to Arkansas, the lawmen felled a tree across Cane Creek ford. When the wagon, swaying and rattling with its load of outlaws, approached the creek, the horses reared to a stop at the obstruction. Lawmen materialized from the woods.

"Throw down those guns," commanded Ledbetter, his cold eye, just above the barrel of his leveled Winchester, bored into Al Jennings' flushed face.

Al Jennings' ego had demanded that he should try to outshine the storied outlaws, and the redhaired ex-lawyer had made a determined effort. However, Al Jennings was no fool. He and his gang members quickly discarded their weapons.

Al Jennings was the last nineteenth-century outlaw of prominence to appear on the Territorial scene. The profession of banditry was becoming highly unprofitable, and the long memory of the federal law permitted no rest for past offenders. Deputy marshals Charley Copeland and Enos Mills patiently tracked down clues involving Arch Wolf, who had escaped the ruined fort at the height of the Christie battle. Securing a lead, Copeland and Mills went to Chicago and located Wolf in the lobby of a hotel. The wanted man was reading a newspaper, and the two marshals simply stood in front of him with drawn six guns. The astonished Wolf surrendered as hastily as possible.

When the turn of the century appeared on calendars, even the topography of the Indian Territory began changing rapidly. The more the violent era waned, the greater became the flow of settlers. Railroads began probing sections that once were remote, and vast new areas were opened for habitation.

Meanwhile, Paden Tolbert's home town was jolted from a decade of peacefulness.

Sheriff John Powers had carried out to the letter the law enforcement principles of Bud McConnell. History can never record how many additional terms Powers would have served in his office, for on the night of February 5, 1902, four bandits set off a charge of explosives in the

Bank of Clarksville. Awakened by the blast, Sheriff Powers rushed to the scene and accosted the startled robbers. In a heated gun battle with one outlaw the sheriff was mortally wounded, and the bandits escaped.

Following a gloomy journey to Clarksville for the funeral of their former comrade, Paden Tolbert and Bud Ledbetter had consolation in witnessing the tremendous popularity of Sheriff Johnny Powers. The citizens of Clarksville immediately conscripted $1500 for a gigantic monument. It would be by far the largest tombstone in Oakland Cemetery.

Nearly a year later three of the bandits were caught, and their public hangings marked the last gallows punishment in Johnson County. Deputy Marshal Paden Tolbert sensed the ending of an epic era.

In the Indian Territory further events of 1902 served as a balm for the bitter memories of outlaw days. Oil discoveries constituted the big news. With increasing tempo, black magic from the bowels of the earth was spewing through the timbers of hastily constructed derricks. The boom was on.

The twentieth-century oil boom changed the Indian Territory almost overnight. New customs, towns and people supplanted the old frontier way of life. In 1907 history absorbed the Territory when Oklahoma became the forty-sixth state of the Union. The large number of federal lawmen dwindled away. Some sought the newly created county law enforcement jobs, others became railroad guards, and some sought new occupations. Even the usefulness of the faithful horse was about to be curtailed. "Automation," in the form of horseless carriage playthings of the oil barons, began appearing on Oklahoma roads.

The Era of Judge Parker, and the men who rode for him, dimmed into the past.

POSTSCRIPT

Perhaps it is a gift some men have that enables them to grasp fundamental changes in a way of life. Certainly, Martin Luther Stoufer was one of the few men of his day who realized that the dread old gallows at Fort Smith would eventually become a part of history.

Shortly after the death of Judge Parker, Stoufer obtained a contract to demolish the gallows that he had built in the eighties. Ignoring the clammy superstition that surrounded the gibbet, he hauled away most of the heavy timbers and utilized them for fuel in the steam power system of his large woodworking plant. However, he saved a piece of oak and used it to carve out a jewelry box for his wife.

Fort Smith citizens silently cheered the passing of the old gallows, and rightly so. The mere fact that there was no longer a need for the grisly structure was a boon to the community. But Stoufer's sense of history was borne out sixty years later. The court of Judge Parker has been restored as a museum, and top attraction at the site is an exact, full scale replica of the monster gallows.

Paden Tolbert's rapport with his changing era was also exemplified by action. He became interested in an exciting new sideline that eventually resulted in a change of career.

Former U. S. Marshal Morton Rutherford had become a prominent attorney at Muskogee. In company with a fellow lawyer, Jesse H. Hill, he contracted with the Fort Smith and Western Railroad to locate townsites. The new railroad was pushing westward from Fort Smith and was capable of spawning towns where likely sites were crossed. The two lawyers had the Creek Nation area and by April 1902, they had established the town of Okemah. Rutherford observed Paden Tolbert's keen interest in the fascinating business of founding towns. Tolbert was little known by press release standards, but he was a familiar and respected figure to hundreds of residents in the area. When braced by Rutherford, Tolbert readily accepted a part-time job. The lawman with southern courtliness performed with the aplomb of a school principal at a faculty reception, aiding the lawyers in securing leases for sale as "town lots."

Shortly after the founding of Okemah, Rutherford and Hill profitably sold their interests to Lake Moore and E. O. Clark of Weleetka, I.T. Tolbert continued working for the new contractors as his law enforcement duties permitted. He moved his family to Weleetka in order to be in the center of the fast-growing area. As rail-bred towns materialized in the wake of the creeping iron tracks, outlaws and anti-social folk were discomfited. They did not appreciate the onslaught of progress in the frontier sections.

One new town however, had a smooth and orderly start for it was only a short distance from Paden Tolbert's new home. There was no "hurrahing" on Main Street, where a deputy U.S. marshal was apt to appear at any moment. As wooden structures began replacing the temporary tents, the suggestion was tendered by the grateful citizens that the unusually peaceful town should be named for Tolbert.

The town fathers were willing, but they faced a problem. Many folks in the Territory pronounced the name "Tolbert" to rhyme with "Colbert." Extant already in the Territory was the town of Colbert, and it was feared that a post office confusion could result by using the name of Tolbert. However, a solution was quickly found. Use the officer's first name! The new town was then christened Paden, and

Deputy Marshal Paden Tolbert became the only lawman in the United States to have a full-fledged town named for him.

Tolbert's love for giant rushing trains finally led him to his third choice of careers. In 1904 he resigned his deputy marshal commission to accept a position of Detective and Claim Agent for the lusty new Fort Smith and Western Railroad. However, the gods that patiently protect veteran lawmen decreed that he would not have a career outside the federal service.

Within four months after assuming the duties of his new job, the mighty frame of Paden Tolbert finally yielded to the rigors imposed by countless nights spent sleeping on the ground, long hours in the saddle during pelting rains and exposure to winter winds. His latent asthma was stirred again and again by his rugged, outdoor way of life. With his physical resistance low, Tolbert contracted a severe case of oak poisoning. His fair skin was aflame with the virulent poison. The maddening pain prompted him to seek relief at the most popular spa in that section of the country. He went to Hot Springs, Arkansas, to "take the waters."

April 24, 1904, Lucy Tolbert received a telegram at her Weleetka home. Her husband had died. Immediate cause of death was attributed to a severe conjestion of the lungs. Lucy and her four children, Mary, Paden, Jr., Louis, and Tom, made their sorrowing trip to the home of J. R. Tolbert at Ludwig. The body of Paden Tolbert was shipped to Clarksville, and he was buried in Oakland Cemetery, April 28.

The citizens of Paden, I.T., did what they could to console the widow. By means of a petition they obtained an appointment for Lucy Tolbert. She moved her brood to Paden and began the duties of postmistress.

The name of Tolbert became well known in Arkansas. Throughout his life in the state, J. R. Tolbert stubbornly persisted with his beloved peach orchard. Tolbert, and other pioneer Johnson County orchardists, sought returns each year on investments of toil and money. It was often as bitter and seemingly uneven a fight as the outlaw versus lawman struggle. Some years saw nature in contrary moods. Early spring warmth would bring out tiny buds on myriad limbs of peach trees. Then, an overnight freeze would doom the dreams of abundant peach crops. In 1899 John Tolbert had yielded his deputy marshal commission in order to aid his aging father. The persistent trial and error methods, and the general increase in fruit-growing knowledge finally paid off for the Tolberts. Today, the name of Tolbert is synonymous in Johnson County with the giant Elberta peach. Peach harvesting is a major industry, and Clarksville proudly proclaims itself as the "Peach Capital of the World."

The twentieth century had passed the halfway mark when Johnson County, aware of the fast-paced changes in industry, agriculture and topography, took a look at its tumultuous, bullet-marked past. Paden Tolbert and his contemporary lawmen had long been relegated to the distant stage where old-timers verbally re-enacted the dramas of long ago. All of the throngs of lawmen who saw service "with Parker" are gone. Walter "Spunky" Taylor died in 1961 in a rest home. Dave Rusk, suffering the consequences of his rugged life, died in 1897 at Siloam Springs, Arkansas. Heck Bruner, whose "side line" was the operation of the old Commercial Hotel at Pryor Creek (Pryor, Oklahoma), met his doom attempting to swim across Grand River in 1902. Big Ed Ratterree died at McAlester, Oklahoma, in 1912. Staunch old G. S. White passed away at Lavita, Colorado, in 1914. Bill Ellis succumbed to cancer at Hartshorne, Oklahoma, in 1920. Charley Copeland fought a losing battle with pneumonia at Drumright, Oklahoma, in 1924. Tom Johnson passed away in Glendale, California, in 1940. John Tolbert died at Clarksville in 1944 and Wess Bowman was a resident in a rest home at Seminole, Oklahoma, when he died in 1957.

Johnson County decided it was time for a review of the old days. October 26, 1958, was designated as Paden Tolbert Day—the county's first frontier celebration. The Johnson County Chamber of Commerce directed all male citizens to begin growing whiskers of the 1890 styles.

It was an important day for Clarksville. The granite marker that had stood for fifty-four years on Tolbert's grave was refurbished. Engravings were entered, listing his deeds while serving as a deputy marshal in Judge Parker's Court.

Clarksville's Mayor Siegel gave the principal address at the celebration that followed, reviewing the dramatic Territorial days:

". . . deputy marshal Paden Tolbert lived by simple, effective principles. Let us hope our own 'frontier' will have equally sturdy principles, and iron men to back them up!"

Bibliography

PRIMARY SOURCES

Aiken, E. C.
Deputy United States marshal, Western District of Arkansas, Fort Smith, Arkansas.

Allard, Lou S.
Editor, *The Drumright Derrick*, Drumright, Oklahoma.

Allen, Orville E.
Son of Deputy Marshal Absolum Allen. Palos Verdes Estates, California.

Atchison, Cecil.
Collector of Judge Parker Museum pieces. Fort Smith, Arkansas.

Ballenger, Dr. T. L.
Emeritus Professor of History, Northeastern State College, Tahlequah, Oklahoma.

Barnes, Ethel.
Niece of Deputy Marshal Gideon S. White. Bartlesville, Oklahoma.

Bates, Earle.
Pioneer resident of Fayetteville, Arkansas.

Belt, Albert Ward.
Pioneer resident of Tahlequah, Oklahoma.

Belt, Autumn McKennon.
Niece of A. S. McKennon—Dawes Indian Commission. Tahlequah, Oklahoma.

Beidleman, George C.
Pioneer attorney of the Indian Territory. Okmulgee, Oklahoma.

Birch, David R.
Pioneer railroadman, Frisco Railroads. Tulsa, Oklahoma.

Blackard, Ed. D.
Arkansas State Police, nephew of Paden Tolbert. Van Buren, Arkansas.

Blackard, Ella.
Sister of posseman Oscar Blackard. Clarksville, Arkansas.

Blackard, Mary Estelle (Stella).
Sister of Paden and John Tolbert. Houston, Texas.

Bogle, James.
Student of schoolteacher (Deputy Marshal) G. S. White. Six Mile
Bend (Spavinaw), Oklahoma.

Bombarger, Mrs. C. C.
Pioneer resident of Paden, Oklahoma.

Bond, Mrs. Ed.
Daughter of Deputy Marshal L. P. Isbel. Vinita, Oklahoma.

Bowman, Omer.
Son of Deputy Marshal Wess Bowman. Seminole, Oklahoma.

Bowman, Mrs. Wess.
Wife of Deputy Marshal Wess Bowman. Wetumka, Oklahoma.

Bushyhead, Dennis W.
Son of Dennis Bushyhead, Principal Chief of the Cherokee Nation in
the days of Ned Christie. Westville, Oklahoma.

Bragg, Mrs. L. E.
Niece of Deputy Marshal Heck Bruner. Tulsa, Oklahoma.

Bristow, George.
Pioneer resident of the Indian Territory and free lance writer. Ozark,
Arkansas.

Carmichael, Eleanor.
Niece of Deputy Marshal G. S. White. Oak Ridge, Tennessee.

Cheatham, W. L.
Pioneer attorney of the Indian Territory. Bristow, Oklahoma.

Clark, Nora T.
Johnson County Historical Society. Clarksville, Arkansas.

Copeland, Walter.
Brother of Deputy Marshal Charles E. Copeland. Welch, Oklahoma.

Cooney, Dora Ratterree.
Daughter of Deputy Marshal Ed. B. Ratterree. McAlester, Oklahoma.

Cottle, Al.
Chief deputy marshal (RTN). Tulsa, Oklahoma.

Crabtree, O. W.
Pioneer resident of the Indian Territory. Pryor, Oklahoma.

Davies, Ada Hilton.
Poet and journalist. San Francisco, California.

Davis, Ira.
Pioneer resident of Paden, I.T. Sand Springs, Oklahoma.

Devault, Roy E.
Collector, period picture frames. Tulsa, Oklahoma.

Donnell, Eileen Tolbert.
Niece of Deputy Marshal Paden Tolbert. Clarksville, Arkansas.

Ellis, Aubie.
Wife of Deputy Marshal William Ellis. Wetumka, Oklahoma.

Elms, Tommy.
Pioneer resident of Summers, Arkansas.

Farmer, Lee.
Pioneer resident of Clarksville, Arkansas.

Felkins, Margaret Blackard.
Niece of Deputy Marshal Paden Tolbert. Clarksville, Arkansas.

Foreman, Carolyn Thomas.
Historian and author. Muskogee, Oklahoma.

Friend, Billy.
Pioneer cowboy of the Indian Territory. Vinita, Oklahoma.

Goff, Mollie Rusk.
Daughter of Deputy Marshal David Vancel Rusk. Skiatook, Oklahoma.

Good, Mary Elizabeth.
Photojournalist and historian. Tulsa, Oklahoma.

Gordon, Nanah E.
Deputy United States marshal, Western District of Arkansas. Fort Smith, Arkansas.

Gray, Walter.
Pioneer resident of Paden, I.T. Hartshorne, Oklahoma.

Hatch, Mary Smith.
Daughter of Deputy Marshal William C. Smith. Tulsa, Oklahoma.

Harp, Hugh.
Deputy marshal of the Judge Parker Era. Van Buren, Arkansas.

Harvey, Bess.
Niece of Marshal John N. Sarber. Clarksville, Arkansas.

Hightower, Jess M.
Manager, Public Relations, Douglas Aircraft Company. Tulsa, Oklahoma.

Hill, Jesse H.
Pioneer attorney of the Indian Territory. Tulsa, Oklahoma.

Hathorne, Ione Blackard.
Niece of Deputy Marshal Paden Tolbert. Houston, Texas.

Hoge, Bill.
Columnist, *The Tulsa World*. Collinsville, Oklahoma.

Hopper, Kermit L.
Ballad and folk singer. Tulsa, Oklahoma.

Jett, A. L.
Son of Sheriff W. L. Jett. Knoxville, Arkansas.

Johnson, Clint.
Son of Deputy Marshal Tom Johnson. Tahlequah, Oklahoma.

Jones, Alice.
Granddaughter of Marshal John N. Sarber. Hollywood, California.

Jones, Beatrice.
Granddaughter of Deputy Marshal Dan Maples. Bentonville, Arkansas.

Jones, Lucille R.
Daughter of Marshal John N. Sarber. Hollywood, California.

Knight, Ben, Jr.
Son of Cherokee Lighthorseman Ben Knight. Tahlequah, Oklahoma.

Lackey, Vinson.
Historian and author. Tulsa, Oklahoma.

Langston, J. Argyle.
Nephew of Deputy Marshal G. S. White. Rockledge, Florida.

Lempke, Walter J.
Editor, Washington County Historical Society *Flashbacks*. Fayetteville, Arkansas.

May, Emory.
Missouri Pacific Railroad Conductor (RTN). Clarksville, Arkansas.

McColm, Frank H.
Gun Collector. Loveland, Colorado.

McConnell, F. M.
Pioneer resident of West Fork. Fayetteville, Arkansas.

McGinty, Billy.
Pioneer cowboy of the Indian Territory. Ripley, Oklahoma.

McKennon, Paul.
Pioneer attorney of Clarksville, Arkansas.

Metzger, Kenneth E.
Former Muskogee oil driller. Tulsa, Oklahoma.

Mickel, Lillian.
Photograph collections.
Johnson County Historical Society. Clarksville, Arkansas.

Misch, Fannie.
Historian and author. Tulsa, Oklahoma.

Miller, Mrs. Dick.
Pioneer resident of Poteau, I.T. Poteau, Oklahoma.

Miller, Sally.
Pioneer resident of Clarksville, Arkansas.

Mills, A. D.
Son of Deputy Marshal Enos Mills. Amarillo, Texas.

Mills, E. W.
Son of Deputy Marshal Enos Mills. Sand Springs, Oklahoma.

Norris, Erma M.
Leflore County Sun. Poteau, Oklahoma.

Murphy, Lucille L.
Librarian, The College of the Ozarks. Clarksville, Arkansas.

Owen, W. L.
Deputy marshal, Central District of Oklahoma. Muskogee, Oklahoma.

Park, Ola.
Pioneer resident of Clarksville, Arkansas.

Parks, Lee F., Jr.
Former resident of Muskogee, Oklahoma. Tulsa, Oklahoma.

Parker, Ike C.
Grandson of Judge Isaac C. Parker. Tulsa, Oklahoma.

Pennington, Ben.
Pioneer resident of Clarksville, Arkansas.

Phillips, Mrs. G. R.
Daughter of Deputy Marshal Barney Connelley. Siloam Springs, Arkansas.

Poynor, Francis Q.
Son-in-law of E. T. "Bud" McConnell. Clarksville, Arkansas.

Poynor, Maude McConnell.
Daughter of Bud McConnell. Clarksville, Arkansas.

Ratterree, W. E.
Nephew of Deputy Marshal Ed. B. Ratterree. Gilmore, Oklahoma.

Rector, Gertrude.
Grandniece of Lighthorseman Ben Knight. Stillwell, Oklahoma.

Reif, Hugh.
Grandson of Deputy Marshal James Birkitt. West Fork, Arkansas.

Robinson, Bill.
Pioneer resident of West Fork. Springdale, Arkansas.

Robinson, Sam.
Pioneer resident of West Fork, Arkansas.

Ross, Margaret.
Editor, "The Chronicles of Arkansas," *The Arkansas Gazette,* Little Rock, Arkansas.

Rutherford, S. Morton.
Son of Marshal Morton Rutherford. Tulsa, Oklahoma.

Sarber, Harry.
Grandson of Marshal J. N. Sarber. Ukiah, California.

Shepard, Maude.
Daughter-in-law of Deputy Marshal G. S. White. Vinita, Oklahoma.

Shirley, Glenn.
Historian and author. Stillwater, Oklahoma.

Stahl, T. P.
City Recorder, City of Siloam Springs, Arkansas.

Stevens, Marshall.
Pioneer resident of the Indian Territory. Vinita, Oklahoma.

Summers, J. F.
Son of J. F. Summers. Summers, Arkansas.

Stouffer, Bigler.
Grandson of Martin Luther Stoufer. Tulsa, Oklahoma.

Taylor, Harve.
Pioneer resident of Ludwig, Arkansas.

Taylor, Walter M. "Spunky."
Deputy marshal of the Parker Era. Broken Arrow, Oklahoma.

Taylor, Wess.
Pioneer resident of Ludwig, Arkansas.

Tedmon, Bob S.
Gun collector. Fort Collins, Colorado.

Thompson, Noble.
Son of Deputy Marshal Joe Thompson. Tulsa, Oklahoma.

Thompson, Henry "Blackie."
Pioneer resident of the Indian Territory. Spavinaw, Oklahoma.

Tolbert, Ellanore.
Daughter-in-law of Paden Tolbert. Palatine, Illinois.

Tolbert, Horace.
Nephew of Paden Tolbert. Clarksville, Arkansas.

Tolbert, Mrs. Eugene.
Sister-in-law of Paden Tolbert. Clarksville, Arkansas.

Tolbert, Russell.
Nephew of Paden Tolbert. Clarksville, Arkansas.

Townsend, H. G.
Director of Personnel, Kansas City Southern Railroad Company. Kansas City, Missouri.

Underhill, Bill.
Pioneer resident of West Fork, Arkansas.

Vanzant, George L.
Pioneer resident of the Indian Territory. Inola, Oklahoma.

Watts, Charles G.
Pioneer attorney Fort Smith U. S. Court and the Indian Territory. Wagoner, Oklahoma.

Wenger, Martin.
Librarian, Thomas Gilcrease Institute of American History. Tulsa, Oklahoma.

Westmoreland, Mary Lou.
Sister-in-law of Paden Tolbert. Sallisaw, Oklahoma.

Wiesendanger, Martin W.
Archaeologist, historian, author. Tulsa, Oklahoma.

Williams, Ike.
Pioneer resident of Clarksville, Arkansas.

Wilson, Bill
Tulsa County deputy sheriff. Tulsa, Oklahoma.

SECONDARY SOURCES

1. NEWSPAPERS:

The Arkansas Democrat, Little Rock, Arkansas. July 16, 1927.

The Arkansas Gazette, Little Rock, Arkansas. Feb. 24, 1934, Sept. 25, 1935, March 3, 1958.

The Clarksville Enterprise, Clarksville, Arkansas. July 26, 1873.

The Oklahoma State Capital, Oklahoma City, I.T. Jan. 23, 1903, Feb. 3, 1903, April 29, 1904.

The Daily Oklahoman, Oklahoma City, Oklahoma. June 9, 1918.

The Fort Smith Elevator, Fort Smith, Arkansas. Oct. 12, 1892.

The Herald Democrat, Clarksville, Arkansas. Aug. 25, 1919, Feb. 27, 1930, July 12, 1949, July 24, Oct. 9 and 16, 1958.

The Johnson County Graphic, Clarksville, Arkansas. Aug. 18, 1938, July 8, 1961.

The Johnson County Herald, Clarksville, Arkansas. May 5, 1895, Feb. 5, 1902, April, 1904, January, 1905.

The Muskogee Daily Phoenix, Muskogee, Oklahoma. March 9, 1939.

The Tulsa Tribune, Tulsa, Oklahoma. Oct. 27 and Nov. 29, 1958, June 6, 1959, March 28, 1960, Feb. 19 and 25, 1961.

The Tulsa World, Tulsa, Oklahoma. Dec. 15, 1937, Aug. 5 and Oct. 5, 1952, July 6, 1958.

2. RECORDS AND PERIODICALS:

The Alumni Quarterly, The College of the Ozarks, Clarksville, Arkansas. March 20, 1941.

Development of Oklahoma Territory, E. H. Linzee. Oklahoma City, Oklahoma. 1940.

Johnson County Court Records—1878–86. Clarksville, Arkansas.

Life in Oklahoma, Oklahoma City, Oklahoma. Aug. 1940.

Official Records of the War of the Rebellion, Part 2, Vol. XXII, p. 759. Department of the Missouri, USA.

The Ozark Mountaineer, Springfield, Missouri. Dec. 1958.

Report of the Adjutant General of the State of Arkansas for the Period of the Late Rebellion. Mis. Doc. No. 53, Senate, in the 39th Congress, 2nd session. 1867.

The Sid Wallace Manuscript, Diary of Paul McKennon (unpublished), 1936. Clarksville, Arkansas.

United Confederate Veterans Reunion Program, Sept. 28, 1892. Fort Smith, Arkansas.

U. S. Marshal Office Records, Central District of Oklahoma. Muskogee, Oklahoma.

U. S. Marshal Office Records, Western District of Arkansas. Fort Smith, Arkansas.

3. BOOKS

Douglas, C. B. *The History of Tulsa, Oklahoma,* Vols. 1, 2, and 3, Chicago-Tulsa, The S. J. Clarke Publishing Company, 1921.

Cunningham, Robert E. *Indian Territory,* Norman, Oklahoma, The University of Oklahoma Press, 1957.

Harman, S. W. *Hell on the Border,* Fort Smith, Arkansas, Phoenix Publishing Company, 1898.

Masterson, V. V. *The Katy Railroad and the Last Frontier,* Norman, Oklahoma, University of Oklahoma Press, 1952. 2nd printing, 1953.

McReynolds, Edwin C. *Oklahoma, A History of the Sooner State,* Norman, Oklahoma, The University of Oklahoma Press, 1956.

Reynolds, J. H., and Thomas, David Y. *History of the University of Arkansas,* Fayetteville, Arkansas, University of Arkansas, 1910.

Shirley, Glenn. *Law West of Fort Smith,* New York, Henry Holt and Company, 1957.

———. *Six Gun and Silver Star,* Albuquerque, New Mexico, University of New Mexico Press, 1955.

———. *Heck Thomas, Frontier Marshal,* Philadelphia and New York, Chilton Company, 1962.

INDEX